D1503263

Making Room

A DEVOTIONAL WITH BROOKE NICHOLLS

© 2020 by Brooke Nicholls

Published by Amazon Kindle KDP

All rights reserved. No part of this publication may be reproduced, stored in a retrieval system, or transmitted in any form or by any means – for example, electronic, photocopy, recording – without the prior written permission of the publisher. The only exception is brief quotations in printed reviews.

Cover and layout design by Katrina Robert
Lettering and Illustrations by Emily Leger

Some names with regard to stories in this book have been changed to help protect the privacy of individuals.

Scripture quotations marked (NIV) are taken from the Holy Bible, New International Version®, NIV®. Copyright © 1973, 1978, 1984, 2011 by Biblica, Inc.™ Used by permission of Zondervan. All rights reserved worldwide. www.zondervan.comThe "NIV" and "New International Version" are trademarks registered in the United States Patent and Trademark Office by Biblica, Inc.™

Scripture quotations marked (TPT) are taken from The Passion Translation®. Copyright © 2017, 2018 by Passion & Fire Ministries, Inc. Used by permission. All rights reserved. ThePassionTranslation.com.

Scripture quotations marked (NLT) are taken from the Holy Bible, New Living Translation, copyright ©1996, 2004, 2015 by Tyndale House Foundation. Used by permission of Tyndale House Publishers, a Division of Tyndale House Ministries, Carol Stream, Illinois 60188. All rights reserved.

Scripture quotations marked (ESV) are from The ESV® Bible (The Holy Bible, English Standard Version®), copyright © 2001 by Crossway, a publishing ministry of Good News Publishers. Used by permission. All rights reserved.

Scripture quotations marked (NAS) are taken from the NEW AMERICAN STANDARD (NAS): Scripture taken from the NEW AMERICAN STANDARD BIBLE®, copyright© 1960, 1962, 1963, 1968, 1971, 1972, 1973, 1975, 1977, 1995 by The Lockman Foundation. Used by permission.

Scripture quotations marked (THE VOICE) are taken from THE VOICE (The Voice): Scripture taken from THE VOICE ™. © 2008 by Ecclesia Bible Society. Used by permission. All rights reserved.

Scripture quotations marked (MSG) are taken from THE MESSAGE, © 1993, 2002, 2018 by Eugene H. Peterson. Used by permission of NavPress. All rights reserved. Represented by Tyndale House Publishers, a Division of Tyndale House Ministries.

Scripture quotations marked (NCV) are taken from the NEW CENTURY VERSION (NCV): Scripture taken from the NEW CENTURY VERSION®. © 2005 by Thomas Nelson, Inc. Used by permission. All rights reserved.

Scripture quotations marked (GNB) are taken from the GOOD NEWS BIBLE (GNB): Scriptures taken from the Good News Bible © 1994 published by the Bible Societies/HarperCollins Publishers Ltd UK, Good News Bible© American Bible Society 1966, 1971, 1976, 1992. Used with permission.

Scripture quotations marked (NKJV) are taken from the NEW KING JAMES VERSION (NKJV): Scripture taken from the NEW KING JAMES VERSION®. © 1982 by Thomas Nelson, Inc. Used by permission. All rights reserved.

Scripture quotations marked (KJV) are taken from the KING JAMES VERSION (KJV): KING JAMES VERSION, public domain.

Scripture quotations marked (CSB) are taken from the Christian Standard Bible®, Copyright © 2017 by Holman Bible Publishers. Used by permission. Christian Standard Bible, and CSB® are federally registered trademarks of Holman Bible Publishers.

Scripture quotations marked (CEV) are taken from the CONTEMPORARY ENGLISH VERSION (CEV): Scripture taken from the CONTEMPORARY ENGLISH VERSION © 1995 by the American Bible Society. Used by permission

Scripture quotations marked (AMP) are taken from the Amplified Bible, Copyright © 2015 by The Lockman Foundation. Used by permission.

Cornerstone:
CCLI #6158927
© 2011 Hillsong Music Publishing (Admin. by EMI Christian Music Publishing) All rights reserved.

Way Maker:
CCLI #7115744
Osinachi Okoro
© 2016 Integrity Music Europe (Admin by Capitol CMG Publishing) All Rights Reserved.

10,000 Reasons:
CCLI #6016351
© 2011 SHOUT! PUBLISHING (ASCAP), sixsteps Music (ASCAP), SAID AND DONE MUSIC (ASCAP) and THANKYOU MUSIC (PRS) SHOUT! PUBLISHING Admin. in the United States and Canada at EMICMGPUBLISHING.COM sixsteps Music and SAID AND DONE MUSIC Admin. at EMICMGPUBLISHING.COM THANKYOU MUSIC Admin. Worldwide at EMICMGPUBLISHING.COM excluding Europe which is Admin. at Kingswaysongs.
All Rights Reserved.

Never Once:
CCLI #5997055
© 2011 Thankyou Music (PRS) (adm. worldwide at CapitolCMGPublishing.com excluding Europe which is adm. by Integrity Music, part of the David C Cook family. Songs@integritymusic.com) / worshiptogether.com Songs (ASCAP) sixsteps Music (ASCAP) (adm. at CapitolCMGPublishing.com) / Windsor Hill Music () / Spirit Nashville Three () / So Essential Tunes (SESAC) / Bmg Chrysalis () All rights reserved.

Who You Say I Am:
CCLI #7102401
Ben Fielding, Reuben Morgan
© 2018 Hillsong Music Publishing (Admin by Capitol CMG Publishing) All rights reserved.

So Will I (100 Billion X):
CCLI #7084123
© 2017 Hillsong Music Publishing (APRA) (adm. in the US and Canada at CapitolCMGPublishing.com) All rights reserved.

ENDORSEMENTS FOR 'MAKING ROOM'

"Brooke offers us in print what she so graciously gives in worship—her whole self. Honest, authentic, deeply hopeful and practically based, Brooke is inviting us to real connection and intentional intimacy— 'Making Room' is a doorway to God."
– *Danielle Strickland, Speaker, Author, Advocate*

"Brooke offers very personal and biblical landscapes for the soul in her new book, 'Making Room'. Each devotion is a restorative pause in the midst of busy-ness and distraction. Having watched her walk with God over the years, I trust her insights and encouragement. You will too."
– *Paul Baloche, Worship Leader and Three-time Dove Award Winning Songwriter*

"Brooke brings her heart and soul to this devotional. It is sure to be a gift to all who pick it up."
– *Carey Nieuwhof, Bestselling Author, Podcaster and Speaker*

"'Making Room' is a rich blend of Scripture, spiritual practices and real life reflections that model vulnerability and the way of Christ. Thank you Brooke for giving us a welcoming place to meet with Jesus."
– *Bruxy Cavey, Teaching Pastor of The Meeting House and author of Best Seller "The End of Religion" and "(re)union: the Good News of Jesus for Seekers, Saints, and Sinners'*

"I love the way Brooke leads worship. She doesn't just invite us to sing, but invites us to join her in the victory, breakthrough and freedom she has experienced in Jesus Christ. And Brooke carries this same kind of invitation into the writing of "Making Room". I'm so excited for you to read her words and be drawn into these beautiful revelations and encouragements of who Jesus is and what He has to offer."

– *Luke Stones, Worship Pastor at GT Church, Royal City Worship*

To the woman who taught me to turn to Scripture before anything else, and to love without limits. Mom, this book is dedicated to you. For my entire life I've watched you give all that you had to those hurting and in need. I've seen you be a mother to the motherless, feed the hungry and clothe the poor. You have been running your race with endurance, with eyes turned to Jesus and you've changed not only my life but the lives of many. You are an incredible woman and I love you with my whole heart. Xx

THANK YOU

A huge thank you to my friend Skye in B.C. If I didn't have a friend like you who was so generous with your time, I wouldn't have finished this book when I did. Despite a three hour time difference, you would wake up at 5am and meet me on FaceTime to help me edit before you started work. Then COVID-19 hit and the trend continued as you encouraged me to keep going when I began to feel drained or discouraged. Skye, thank you for being the one person who cared about this devotional more than me. I'm thankful for every hour you invested into this book– you're the best cheerleader!

Thank you to my sweet friend Jessica for being the very first person I ever confided in when God asked me to do this. Jessica, your support and wisdom pushed me to take my first steps in putting my words to paper. Starting is the hardest part, but because of you, it was made easy. Thank you for helping me with my 'Takeaways' and lending your heart to this project. It wouldn't be what it is today without you. You are an extremely special girl and I'll always remember what you did for me.

To my mom and dad: Thanks for always smiling upon me and believing in everything I put my heart into. My desire for seeing people know Jesus stemmed from when I was just a little girl watching you both set the bar so high and lead by example. I miss you both so much and when quarantine is over, I'm coming home for the world's longest hug!

To my mother- and father-in-law: It's crazy to think that one girl could hit the in-law jackpot so big. But here I am. I feel so cared for and loved by you both, thanks for helping me and encouraging me in this project!

Lastly, Steve: Thanks for being my best friend and greeting me every morning with a coffee and a kiss. There's not a thing in this world that you don't make me feel like I can do (other than play the tambourine on beat) and because of that I am where I am today. You're the greatest gift God could have ever given me. Love you forever!

AUTHOR'S NOTE

In 2018 I felt the Lord asking me to write a devotional and what a journey it has been! As somebody who had struggled with feelings of inadequacy and considered herself academically challenged, I didn't think this venture was for me. But what I've learned through this process is that whatever it is God calls us to do, He gives us the supernatural strength to get through it. But not only to just get through it, to get through it feeling empowered and stronger than when we first started! I admit, there were some serious dry times in my writing and some moments of frustration, but looking back I can see God's hand on every one of those moments.

The craziest thing about finishing this book is that it was unexpectedly finished during the 2020 COVID-19 global pandemic! Who would have thought I'd wake up and out of nowhere have an extra 100 hours to spare? One moment I'm on my way to the Junos, and planning for Nights of Worship and Conferences across Canada and the next thing we know, the entire world is shut down and everybody's lives are put on hold. Can you believe we lived to see this happen!? I'm writing this note while we are all still isolated and quarantined, and although it's been challenging for my husband and I (and *many* others), we've met God in new ways during this pandemic and have been reminded that God really is who He says He is. We've seen Him provide for us and meet us in the most creative and uncanny ways, and these stories of God's faithfulness will be ones that we'll pass down to our children, who will hopefully pass them down to theirs. I imagine this pandemic will be talked about for the rest of all time, and I pray God's faithfulness will be directly linked to it.

I hope that through these pages you can hear the genuineness in my writing with the hope to lift your eyes to Jesus and bring you closer to Him. I wrote these devotionals based on real life experiences, different conversations with people, observations I made throughout my travels and different seasons that God has brought me through. As I edited this book I was able to get a broader scope of even my own heart, which is: to see people come to Jesus with eyes forever fixed on Him, knowing that He is everything they'll ever need in this life, and more.

Thank you for reading and spending time with this book. Your support means everything to both Steve and I. Our life over the years has been one big leap of faith and through it all, we've continued to see God in every area ... and you've played a huge role in that! I hope that one day soon we'll get to gather wherever it is in the world you live to worship and exalt the wonderful name of Jesus together!

God Bless you!

Brooke x

TABLE OF CONTENTS

Making Room

"ENLARGE YOUR TENT AND ADD EXTENSIONS TO YOUR DWELLING."

ISAIAH 54:2 (TPT)

1

At the beginning of the year I heard God tell me to "make room." But, if I'm being transparent here, I wasn't totally sure exactly what that meant. I mean, I thought I was spending enough time in the Word, writing, dreaming and praying. But as I began to dive into what "making room" looked like, I quickly realized that it wasn't about all the time I was putting in, rather, living in active faith and preparation; ready for God to move at any moment.

Some of my dearest friends are in the process of adopting and have known that a little babe would be joining their family for about three years now. They've gone through all the lists, the classes, the in-home case worker visits, the paperwork, etc, etc. Now, after years of waiting, they continue to wait for that one special phone call. But let's say they get that call tomorrow, and their reaction is, "What? Now? We're not prepared!" Could you imagine? What do you mean you're not prepared? You've been hoping, praying and dreaming of this phone call for years…

Do you see where I'm going with this? Many of us have dreams in our hearts and have been praying for restoration, a breakthrough, or that special "phone call" for years, but simply put, are just not ready. We think we'll get ready when it comes, but God is waiting on us to be ready before it comes.

In Isaiah 54 the Lord speaks to the entire country of Israel who were waiting in exile saying, "Israel will be restored like a barren woman who bears many children." But before God actually brings restoration and fulfills His promise, the very first verse in this chapter instructs them to, "Rejoice with singing, you barren one! You who have never given birth, burst into a song of joy and shout…" You see, we tend to do the opposite: rejoice, give thanks and burst into a song of joy *after* our breakthrough. But actually, just like the Israelites, God is calling us to do all of that before our breakthrough, activating our faith and believing that He is a God of His word.

Friends, we need to prepare our hearts for the things to come by actively practicing our faith in who God is. On days when we can't necessarily see those things, we need to trust in the hope and promise that God is working everything out according to His purpose and plan.

Listen to this promise: "Increase is coming, so enlarge your tent and add extensions to your dwelling. Hold nothing back! Make the tent ropes longer and the pegs stronger…" (v.2-3)

This is a call to the people of Israel to *get ready and make room for what God is about to do!* But more than that, I believe this is a word for all of us today. I decided to call this devotional book "Making Room" because God is calling you and I to "make room" for Him to move in our lives and do what only He can do. As we begin to lean into Scripture with new eyes, we open the door for God to reveal Himself to us in new ways. I pray this book would encourage you and change the way you view, live and interact with the Living God. Enlarge your tents today, lift your heart in worship and rejoice in who God is! Activate your faith knowing that God will fulfill His promise in you as you make room for Him to draw close and move!

TAKEAWAY

Do you feel prepared? Have you been waiting for restoration, healing, for your prayers to be answered or for breakthrough? Lift your heart in worship and make a joyful noise to the Lord, activating your faith in who you know God to be. Cling to His Word as you prepare your heart for Him to come do the things that only our mighty God can do! Praying that you'll meet the Lord in a brand new way as you lean in and make room for Him today.

#10: Do Not Covet

"SO WE FIX OUR EYES NOT ON WHAT IS SEEN, BUT ON WHAT IS UNSEEN. FOR WHAT IS SEEN IS TEMPORARY, BUT WHAT IS UNSEEN IS ETERNAL."

2 CORINTHIANS 4:18 (NIV)

If you asked me to rhyme off the 10 commandments to you right now, this is what comes to mind: don't steal, or lie, don't idolize, or take the Lord's name in vain, and keep the sabbath holy. Easy—done, done, and done. But it's the pesky last commandment I forget about and really need to focus on: "Do not covet." Exodus 20:17 (ESV) says, "You shall not covet your neighbour's house; you shall not covet your neighbour's wife, or his male servant, or his female servant, or his ox, or his donkey, or anything that is your neighbour's." Now, the word "covet" means to "yearn to possess or have." Basically it means to want other people's things. With that in mind, here's how I read that verse in the twentieth century:

Don't desire to have that blogger's giant picture-perfect house, don't desire to have their gorgeous, fit husband or wife either, don't desire to have their nanny that looks after their kids or their maid that comes once a week to keep things shiny and in order. Don't desire their expensive cars or vespas... don't desire *anything* that is not yours.

Here's the harsh truth about coveting: it's a universal sin. It's one of those sins that we all struggle with no matter who we are or where we are in life— especially with the internet at our fingertips. It's become too easy to jump online to see all the things, opportunities and abilities people have. And while it's not wrong to dream and aspire for great things, it's wrong to want what other people have. It's a big world out there; somebody will always be doing something cooler, looking more fit, making more money, and will have bigger, better things than you. And when we feast our eyes on other people's lives, we actually forfeit our own joy, causing ourselves to question who God has created us to be and the different lengths He's brought each one of us.

2 Corinthians reminds us to, "fix our eyes not on what is seen, but on what is unseen, since what is seen is temporary, but what is unseen is eternal." Now, the way we process the difference between the things seen and unseen should bring a level of peace and contentment in our hearts, because it's that shift in our perspective (from earthly to heavenly) that takes our hearts from covetousness and anxiety, and brings us back to contentment and peace.

I want to encourage you to give all your comparing and coveting to God; you have so many things to give thanks for, and so many blessings to count. And through the supernatural power that comes from Christ, He will give you the strength to shift your eyes from what is seen to what is unseen, recognizing the glory of His eternal goodness in your life today.

TAKEAWAY

First, ask the Lord to forgive where you've looked to your "neighbour" and desired the life they have. Our life here on earth is temporary– I pray that God would give you a new heavenly perspective, shifting it from the things seen to unseen. And although this life isn't about what we have or the things we've succeeded in, we all have so much to give thanks for. To help align yourself with God's heart, make a list of 10 things in your life that you're grateful for and give Him thanks and glory for each one.

1._____

2._____

3._____

4._____

5._____

6._____

7._____

8._____

9._____

10._____

A Keystone Habit

"AND LET US CONSIDER HOW WE MAY SPUR ONE ANOTHER ON TOWARD LOVE AND GOOD DEEDS, NOT GIVING UP MEETING TOGETHER, AS SOME ARE IN THE HABIT OF DOING, BUT ENCOURAGING ONE ANOTHER..."

HEBREWS 10:24-25 (NIV)

I learned what a keystone *habit* was the other day and it really got me thinking about church, community and all things surrounding that topic. You're probably thinking, "what in the world is a keystone habit?" Okay, let me explain a little. Keystone habits are habits that lead to the development of multiple good habits which start a chain effect in your life, producing a number of positive outcomes.

For example: Setting a goal to run for 20 minutes a day is a keystone habit because from this *one* habit, this could lead to healthier eating, better sleep at night, positive mood change and more energy in your day. Do you see the chain reaction here? Now, where my mind immediately wandered to when I heard this term "keystone habit" was *church*. Because as Christians, going to church on a weekly basis should be a non negotiable. Imagine the ripple across the nation if every Christian made going to church a weekly keystone habit in their life?

Can you see why going to church on a weekly basis would help develop other good habits in your life? Friends, we are *built* for community. God's word makes it very clear that we're not meant to do this life alone and that we need each other for growth and accountability. I've met many christians who don't attend a local church and while I recognize that it can be hard for some of us to commit to community, especially if we're guarded or have been hurt in the past, *community is God's desire for us*.

Proverbs 27:17 (NIV) tells us that, "As iron sharpens iron, so one person sharpens another."

1 Thessalonians 5:11 (NIV) says, "Therefore encourage one another and build each other up…"

Galatians 6:2 (NIV) tells us to, "Carry each other's burdens, and in this way you will fulfill the law of Christ."

Hebrews 10:24-25 (NIV) says, "And let us consider how we may spur one another on toward love and good deeds, not giving up meeting together, as some are in the habit of doing, but encouraging one another..."

Now I know some of you are thinking, "but church isn't the building, it's the people." And while I agree with that statement, I want to remind you that when we make attending church a priority in our life, the rest follows. Like community, a deeper understanding of who Jesus is found in the bigger picture of the body, and a profound strengthening in your spiritual life as you walk in obedience to God, are just a few habits out of *many* that come from making attending church a keystone habit in your life.

Your community is found in the church, which plays a vital role in your life as a Christian. Do you have people in your life that sharpen you and push you forward? Do you have a community of people that spur you on, encourage you in your dreams but also show up on your doorstep when you've had the unimaginable happen? When the weight of the world is keeping you isolated and fear has become the slave driver in your life, is your community laying hands on you to pray for hope and healing? God's given us all a choice when it comes to choosing what keystone habits we want to mark our lives with. So, I pray that today you would be challenged to choose and implement the right keystone habits for your life, bringing you into a closer relationship with Jesus.

TAKEAWAY

Now that you have an understanding of what keystone habits are, can you identify any in your life right now? Are you a daily jogger?

An early riser? An avid big breakfast eater? Of course there are certain exceptions to the rules here, but what do you consider yourself disciplined in, no matter the circumstance?

Write them down on the lines below:

_____

_____

_____

Now, ask the Holy Spirit to reveal to you one other keystone habit that you could incorporate into your life that would bring you closer into a relationship with Jesus.

_____

_____

I am Free

"SURELY HE TOOK UP OUR PAIN AND BORE OUR
SUFFERING [...] HE WAS PIERCED FOR OUR
TRANSGRESSIONS, HE WAS CRUSHED FOR OUR
INIQUITIES; THE PUNISHMENT THAT BROUGHT
US PEACE WAS ON HIM, AND BY HIS WOUNDS
WE ARE HEALED."

ISAIAH 53:4-5 (NIV)

It was a dark Wednesday night and as I sat at my piano I could hear the cars driving up and down the streets from the 8th floor of my condo. With my bible lying to the right of me, and my notebook to the left, I asked the Lord what song He wanted me to write. My heart had shifted and all I wanted was to be in ministry, sharing God's love through worship. But all I felt was shame, and all I could think was, "how could a girl with a past like mine ever work in ministry?" Shame was wrapping itself around my body like ivy to a trellis. It was keeping me from stepping out into the life God was calling me to, and, in turn holding me back from sharing about the healing and hope that God had so graciously given to me. Shame is a heavy burden, and I had been carrying the load for years.

That night, desperate for freedom through Jesus, the Lord led me to Isaiah 53:4,5 where it reads, "surely He took up our pain and bore our suffering [...] He was pierced for our transgressions, He was crushed for our iniquities; the punishment that brought us peace was upon Him, and by His wounds we are healed." I sat and wept as I read Isaiah, because it was that night that the Holy Spirit revealed to my heart that Jesus actually paid the ultimate price for *me*. It's a funny thing to hear something your whole life but have it take on new meaning in a moment all alone, in a tiny condo. Wow, Jesus took on *my* pain and bore *my* sin so that I wouldn't have to. And the good news is, He did it for you too. He died on the cross for your sins to show you how much He loved you, and He took your shame so that you wouldn't have to live in it or be bound to your past anymore. He paid the price in full; this was the night my eyes were opened and His truth came alive in me.

You see, shame tells us we're guilty and insufficient, but Jesus says we're guiltless and promises that His grace will be sufficient for us in all of our weaknesses.

The things we once said, did, or experienced have been forgiven. In Christ, we are a new creation. God's love frees us to let go of the mess of the past and move forward in confidence, knowing "there is now no condemnation for those who are in Christ Jesus" (Romans 8:1, NIV). Even as I type this, I can feel the truth of who God is, wanting to redeem you and heal you of the shame that holds you back from living the life He's called you to, just like He did me. I pray that as you lean into Jesus, you will experience freedom through the One who promises it. Your story isn't finished! As you surrender your life over to Him, seeking His love and His redemption, I believe God will take your past and use what you've been through to point people to Him. That's who our God is, He takes messy lives and transforms them into beautiful stories.

Today, I am praying for freedom from the things that hold you back, things that keep you hidden in the dark, and that surround you in shame. Jesus paid the price for *you*. You, specifically, were bought by the blood of the King and He wants *you* to live a full life of freedom through Him! Your redemption story will be one that God uses. Surround yourself in His presence as He heals you from the inside out.

TAKEAWAY

Sometimes we can be quick to read Scripture in an auto-pilot mode where we read it, but don't fully comprehend its revelation. King Jesus died for you that day at Calvary! By God's grace, Jesus dying for you is just the beginning. As if that isn't enough,

He wants to restore you, redeem you, transform you, love you, walk with you, care for you, talk with you, hold you, lead you, heal you, comfort you, teach you, and do so much more. May you throw off the chains holding you back and let God take you from glory to glory.

I am free,
bought by the
blood of the King
Jesus laid His life
down for me, broke
the chains that bound
and rescued me
so that I could live
free

I AM FREE

[BROOKE NICHOLLS]

A Ripple Into Eternity

"LET US NOT BECOME WEARY IN DOING GOOD, FOR
AT THE PROPER TIME WE WILL REAP A HARVEST
IF WE DO NOT GIVE UP."

GALATIANS 6:9 (NIV)

I met Celeste at a local bar one weekend while I was pouring my heart out over love songs on my keyboard. By the looks of her tattoos and enthusiasm to cheer me on, she loved music as much as I did. She came over and introduced herself after my set and we chatted about all things music for the majority of the night. We exchanged numbers, and basically, the rest is history.

Growing up I always wanted to lead somebody to Jesus, but truthfully, I had no idea where to even begin. I heard radical stories from people who led their waitress to Jesus in the middle of a shift, or how a dangerous bike gang got saved while robbing a Christian family at a bonfire, and my favourite: leading a flight attendant to Jesus in the middle of a flight. These stories seem so unattainable to me because if I'm being honest with you, the way I share Jesus with people sounds so different from all of these stories.

Everyone's story and testimony about how they came to know Jesus is special and unique to them. So, I simply asked the Lord to show me how I could be a part of somebody's story one day, and in the most direct way He whispered, "invite them…" Here I was thinking that this needed to be some grandiose gesture, when really, God was reminding me that it's His kindness in us that will draw people to Him.

So, I invited Celeste to church. I quickly realized that that first invite was a step in the right direction to opening the door for her to hear the good news of the gospel. And as it would turn out, she said no, but as my courage began to rise I continued to invite her.

Colossians 1:6 (NLT) says, "This same Good News that came to you is going out all over the world. It is bearing fruit everywhere by changing lives, just as it changed your lives from the day you first heard and understood the truth about God's wonderful grace." A life transformed for the Kingdom brings about fruit that feeds the mouths of those starving. In other words: There is power in your invitation.

When somebody is changed by the gospel, they can't help but share their hope with the world around them. I understand it can feel tiresome to ask and ask and then ask again, but the Bible encourages us to not grow weary of doing good; so when you feel like this might be your last ask, don't grow weary, ask again!

After six months of building a friendship with Celeste and inviting her to church, she finally came. (PRAISE GOD!) She ended up giving her life to Jesus and shortly after, made the decision to get baptized. Later on, she began serving in the youth ministry and to this day she continues to spend her free time volunteering however she can at her local church. She shares the good news of Jesus with her clients at work, in the line up at Starbucks, and even on the streets of her city.

Your invitation has an eternal ripple effect. It's a life transformed by the love of Christ, *multiplied*. Never ever underestimate your invitation. God's love and kindness pursue us daily. He never stops inviting us into a relationship with him and He doesn't get annoyed by extending grace to us day after day. Together, let us never stop pursuing the lost, longing for them to meet the Jesus we know and serve.

TAKEAWAY

Write down the names of two people that you need to invite to church. Don't let fear, timidness or embarrassment cripple you. Rather, pray for the Holy Spirit to ignite your heart into action, believing for the eternal ripple effect that one simple invitation can have. Praying for you today as you step out to invest and invite. What an honour it is to be a part of somebody's story.

"AS IRON SHARPENS IRON, SO ONE PERSON
SHARPENS ANOTHER."

PROVERBS 27:17 (NIV)

I grew up going to a small Bible camp two hours east of my hometown. Every July my mom would pack our bags and we'd spend four weeks of our summer at camp: attending services, eating ice cream, biking until sunset and well, meeting my best friends.

Fast forward 17 years and five besties later. I can honestly say we've been through pretty much everything together: marriages, babies, career changes, panic attacks, miscarriages, divorces you name it. We've been there for one another in the crazy and in the unexpected and what I've learned is that all friendships, no matter the length or lessons learned throughout, are a gift from God. While some are meant to last a lifetime, others are only meant for certain seasons or specific reasons.

Losing friends can be painful, especially if the breakup wasn't mutual. I've travelled that road of unexpectedly losing a deep friendship, and man did it hurt. But God in His mercy, saw the vacant space in my heart mourning the death of a friend and filled it with His love and His compassion. And He wants to do the same for you.

There's wisdom in seeking out healthy community and there's abundant joy in lasting friendships. King Solomon recognized the power of partnership when he said in Ecclesiastes 4:9 (NIV), "two are better than one, because they have good return for their labour." Basically, we're stronger together than when we are apart. Having those close by, call in the middle of the night, spill your heart out over copious amounts of chocolate kind of friends are necessary. Like, *very* necessary.

But guess what else is necessary? Letting go. Sometimes relationships run their course, and that's okay too! The truth is, some friendships aren't meant to last forever. It doesn't mean they were fake or invalid, but that they were meant to serve a purpose for a reason or season. We have the choice to be bitter and resentful, or to thank God for the gift of friendship in that season; trusting He will provide somebody else to come alongside you in His perfect timing.

Proverbs 27 says, "As iron sharpens iron, so one person sharpens another." I want to encourage you to seek healthy friendships for your life. Friendships that build one another, sharpen one another and carry one another, while remembering that sometimes it's necessary, and healthy, to let go.

But let's be real here, letting go is hard. Finding the gifts amidst pain is hard. Realizing a relationship has moved in a different direction is hard and saying goodbye is hard. Philippians 3:13 (TPT) tells us to "let go of the past and fasten your heart to the future instead." If you've been praying for deep friendships and community, I pray you would fasten your heart to God and be filled with hope for the future as He begins to bring new people into your life. So, whether you've had friends for 15+ years or have experienced loss around friendships, I pray God would answer whatever prayer is deep in your heart during this season. And if you're feeling the weight of letting go, I pray you would be filled with wisdom in taking the next right steps. Be encouraged today in knowing that both of these things are okay, and when done right, are a gift from God.

TAKEAWAY

First, take a moment to give thanks for the friendships that sharpen you and bring you joy. What a gift! Now, let's ask God if there's somebody you're holding onto in an unhealthy way that He is asking you to let go of. Or vice versa, is there somebody in your life that you may need to have a difficult conversation with? Perhaps you're in need of a friend today, take your prayer request to the Lord and trust that His timing is perfect and He will replenish your heart with the right friend for you.

yesterday, today and Forever

"JESUS, THE ANOINTED ONE, IS ALWAYS THE SAME
—YESTERDAY, TODAY, AND FOREVER."

HEBREWS 13:8 (TPT)

As a kid, I grew up going to a Festival called 'Kingdom Bound' at Six Flags in Buffalo, New York. My parents would pack up our white Chrysler LHS and we'd make the four-hour trek across the border to hit up some rides and hear our favourite Christian artists that year. I loved the hype of screaming on roller coasters but I always loved worshipping with everyone way more, so I made sure that my rollercoaster schedule never interfered with who I wanted to hear that day. There was this one particular worship leader who I loved and listened to a lot– his name was Jason Upton. He kind of became popular around the time that I fell in love with worship music and made 'Shout to The Lord' my teenage anthem. Sadly, Darlene Zschech wasn't at Kingdom Bound that year, but when I saw Jason Upton's name on the schedule I was pummmmmped!

I remember that day like it was yesterday. I hadn't stood in front of many people of his caliber at that point in my life and truthfully, I had no idea what I was in for. The tent he was playing in was at capacity, there was literally nowhere for me to sit, so I hung out at the back, tightly packed between hundreds of others who were just as excited as me. As he led us into worship, people began lifting their voices and hands all over the place– people were dancing, falling on their faces and were having encounters with the Holy Spirit; it was a presence that you could practically *taste*. I had never seen anything like this before... people were experiencing Jesus in a way I never even knew existed. This day forever changed the way I knew and viewed Jesus; this was the day that the Lord came down from heaven *revealed Himself to me.*

Life can be hard, and at some point or another we've all been faced with trials and troubles. Hebrews 13:8 says that, "Jesus is the

27

same—yesterday, today, and forever." Maybe you're wondering, "*how does Jesus being the same apply to the terrible circumstances and the hardships that I've faced?*" Well, I wondered the same when the Lord prompted me to write this devotional. And even now as I type, this verse gives me hope in knowing that the same God who met me in that tent all those years ago is the *same* God who *still* meets me now... exactly where I am: broken and fragile, worn and weathered, tired and messy.

As we get older it's easy to become jaded and forget all the times that God met us in our need; providing for us, loving us and comforting us in a way that *only* He could. The same God who performed miracles by turning water into wine is the *same* God who wants to perform miracles in your life today. And believe it or not, the same God who multiplied 2 fish and a loaf of bread to feed 5,000 people is the *same* God who wants to take what you have to offer and multiply it too. And you guessed it, the same God that healed blind eyes and deaf ears wants to meet you today with that *same* healing and hope.

Friends, the work of God isn't limited to one particular time in history. From the stories found in Scripture, to my encounter with God at the age of 14, to this *very* day, He has remained, remains, and will continue to remain the same. He hasn't changed over these years and He still longs to meet with us, to be in relationship with us, to love us and to help us; God wants to do the unimaginable in our lives!   Ephesians 3:20 (NIV) says, "...to Him who is able to do immeasurably more than all we ask or imagine, according to His power that is at work within us." What is it that God has done before in your life? And do you trust that He can do it again? Take heart in knowing that He is the same... yesterday, today and forever.

TAKEAWAY

I'm here to remind you, that you— right where you are, exactly as you are and whatever age that you are— can count on God. The same God that meets you in your successes and joys is the same God that meets you in your let downs and broken dreams. He's the God of your valleys and the God of your mountains... He is the same forever and always, and the things that He's done before He can and will do again.

Way Maker

"I AM THE LORD, WHO OPENED A WAY THROUGH THE WATERS, MAKING A DRY PATH THROUGH THE SEA."

ISAIAH 43:16 (NLT)

After 20 years of marriage and three children later, Kari and her husband separated. They split with the intent to reconcile but as time passed, things became ugly and before she knew it, she was served with divorce papers.

We all know that we should trust the Lord when the waters rage, but why does that feel so hard to do when situations go awry and fall out of our control? We then find ourselves in a constant state of wondering: Why did this thing happen to me? What's God going to do about it? How is He going to do it? And when will He do it?

Throughout the Bible we see many examples of God showing us that when things seem impossible to our human understanding, through Him, *anything* is possible. Maybe you've been in, or currently are in Kari's shoes, so you feel the weight of this story in a deep way. I want to remind you that when all hope is lost, when your situations are all consuming and overwhelming, when you're worried, doubtful or anxious for the future, *God can make a way*.

After a year of being separated and just days before Kari's court appearance, God gave her husband a vision. Long story short, through her husband's obedience to the vision, they reconciled. Can you believe it? Just when things couldn't get any worse, and there seemed to be no hope or future for this marriage, God came swooping in making a way for this beloved family. What a miracle! This reconciliation didn't happen by coincidence though, it happened because in the thick of the impossible, God did what only He could do… He made a way.

Isaiah 43:16,19 (NLT) says, "*I am the Lord, who opened a way through the waters, making a dry path through the sea...I am*

31

making a way in the wilderness and streams in the wasteland." Time and time again, God carries us through the hardships and unknowns of life. He takes us out of the miry pit and gives us a firm place to stand, giving us wells of spring water in the wilderness, and carving paths through the sea for us to walk through. When the waters rage and the thunder roars, our assurance as Christians is found in God who makes a way, where there seems to be no way. I pray that you would feel God's presence surrounding you in whatever it is you're facing, knowing that your prayers for the impossible don't go unheard. Although Kari's story is a unique one, I'm encouraged to know that God was at work from the very beginning. Take heart as you trust the God of all possibilities today!

TAKEAWAY

Is there an area in your life that you need to be reminded of that God is at work and is making a way? Although you may not see it or feel it, God is working things out according to His purpose and plan for your life. To quote my friend, Leeland, "He is the way maker, miracle worker, promise keeper, light in the darkness." He is the One who is on your side, the eternal, all-powerful, ever present God who makes a way for you and I. And I pray that you would find hope in knowing that when things feel too far gone, too broken or too impossible, our God can make *anything* possible, because that's who He is!

Way maker
Miracle worker
promise keeper
light in the darkness
My God, that is
who you are

WAY MAKER

[SINACH]

Align Our Hearts

"HOLD ON TO LOYAL LOVE AND DON'T LET GO, AND BE FAITHFUL TO ALL THAT YOU'VE BEEN TAUGHT. LET YOUR LIFE BE SHAPED BY INTEGRITY, WITH TRUTH WRITTEN UPON YOUR HEART."

PROVERBS 3:3-6 (TPT)

I recently sat in a group of people and listened to a man say, "*God doesn't have a purpose or plan for everybody.*" I'd be lying if I said my mouth didn't drop to the floor, along with my heart for this man's understanding of who God is. During the conversation he said that he had been on his hands and knees praying and fasting for his dreams to come to fruition. After not seeing those dreams come about, he made the decision that God doesn't have plans or a purpose for everybody. Rather, God only has plans for *some* of us.

It breaks my heart to think that anybody would peg God as someone who picks favourites, playing cruel jokes and leaving us to sit in our broken dreams. I'm sorry to that man for the dreams that never came about, but it feels awfully unfair to point the finger at God making a claim like he did. God loves us all with a radical love and he most certainly has *great* plans and purposes for every single one of us.

We all have dreams in our heart. Dreams to want, to have, and to be. But not all the dreams that we have necessarily line up with God's plan for our lives. For example: Not everybody is meant to be a rock star traveling the world one city at a time, even if that's been a dream in your heart since you were seven years old. Some families are called to adopt and some families are called to foster; being a parent might look different than what you imagined. And while some people are called to third world countries for missions, others are called to be missionaries in their own office spaces. Okay, I think you get the point... God actually sees the bigger picture of our lives. So when we pray for the desires of our hearts, we need to surrender our dreams while laying down any and all expectations of what we think our life should look like, asking the Lord to open our eyes to the wonder of *His* ways, not ours. In

35

Proverbs 3:3 (TPT) God says, "follow closely every truth that I've given you. Then you will have a full, rewarding life. Hold on to loyal love and don't let go, and be faithful to all that you've been taught. Let your life be shaped by integrity, with truth written upon your heart." Sometimes God gives us our dreams as they line up with His heart and sometimes He closes doors that lead to destruction. In order to understand where God is leading us, we need to follow the truths that He's given us, by being faithful to His Word and allowing our lives to be shaped by integrity.

I've learned that when we put false expectations on our lives, we also put them on who God is and end up believing false truths like: "God has favourites and only has plans for certain people's lives." When we think or say things like this, we end up putting God in a box and limit who He actually is. I want you to know today that God has a plan and purpose for each one of us, but we need to accept that each call and purpose will look different from one to the other. Will you surrender your understanding, or lack thereof, to God? Instead of being shaken by the collapsing of our false expectations and limited ideas of who God is, let's stand in the truth that our God goes far beyond what we could ever hope or imagine. Trust that He knows what is best for your life, while surrendering every dream and desire buried deep down in your heart today.

TAKEAWAY

Grab your journal, make a list of the dreams that you've been holding onto for some time now. Ask the Lord if there are any dreams on your list that aren't from Him. What are you holding onto that God is asking you to lay down? What do you need to surrender? Pray that your dreams would align with His and that your eyes would be open to where He wants to take you. God has a beautiful purpose and plan for you and He sees every dream in your heart – keep your eyes on Him.

True Repentance

"CHANGE YOUR LIFE, NOT JUST YOUR CLOTHES. COME BACK TO GOD, YOUR GOD. AND HERE'S WHY: GOD IS KIND AND MERCIFUL. HE TAKES A DEEP BREATH, PUTS UP WITH A LOT, THIS MOST PATIENT GOD, EXTRAVAGANT IN LOVE..."

JOEL 2:13 (MSG)

I read once that one of the biggest barriers to spiritual growth is a lack of true repentance. Now, the dictionary defines the word "repentance" like this: "The activity of reviewing one's actions and feeling remorse or regret for past wrongs, which is accompanied by commitment to and actual actions that show and prove a change for the better." As followers of Jesus, our hope as Christians is to become more and more like Him every day, but how can we do this without true repentance in our lives?

Remorse + actual action = true repentance = holiness = becoming more like Jesus.

Let's be honest with each other for a moment: We all know what it looks like to sin and then pretend everything is pure and holy in our lives. Sin is embarrassing and makes us feel all sorts of shame. And, no matter how much we try to fool God, we simply can't because He knows everything, and one day, we'll be accountable for every single thing we've ever done. Those lies we told, the things we did in secret, or the way we pushed our boundaries with zero fear of *who* God is.

Sin separates us from God, from His heart, His truth and from living a life of freedom.

God is looking for people who show remorse, who are broken over their sin and are willing to change their ways. He wants us to turn from our sin and back to him; and the good news is, because of His kindness and mercy, we can! Joel 2:13 says, "*Change your life, not just your clothes. Come back to God... God is kind and merciful. He takes a deep breath, puts up with a lot, this most patient God, extravagant in love...*" What a beautiful invitation to turn from our sin and come back into the arms of our loving Father. When we rend our hearts and separate ourselves from worldly distractions we allow God to fill us with new promise, hope and direction.

I love how that verse tells us to change our life, not just our clothes. Because let's be real, it's easy to look the part without exposing our heart to those around us, but God... He always knows. And Luke 12:2-3 (MSG) tells us that one day our sin will be exposed: "You can't keep your true self hidden forever; before long you'll be exposed. You can't hide behind a religious mask forever; sooner or later the mask will slip and your true face will be known. You can't whisper one thing in private and preach the opposite in public; the day's coming when those whispers will be repeated all over town." Here's the harsh truth: Sin is sin and although we might be the most generous and caring person, we can still be carrying sin in our hearts. However, the good news for everyone is that God gives graciously to the one who says, 'have mercy on me, a sinner!" (Luke 18:13 MSG)

I encourage you to not stay in the habit of just going through the motions when it comes to repenting. The most important part of repentance is the condition of our heart. But true repentance, like all good things, is a gift from God and if we want to obey the command to tear our hearts away from sin, we need to ask God to give us a repentant heart. It's remorse partnered with action that will bring us closer to Jesus. So, let's not ignore our sin, but instead, deal with it. Bring it to Jesus and allow His forgiveness to remove the sin in your life today.

TAKEAWAY

Ask the Holy Spirit to reveal any sin in your life. Ask Him what He wants you to give up and remember, God sees you and knows you completely; there is nothing you can do to hide from Him or fool Him. He knows your motives and heart better than you do… so be honest. Turning from your sin will bring you closer to Jesus and that in itself will change every area of your life.

LET'S PRAY

Lord, we pray that through the power of the Holy Spirit our eyes would be focused, our feet directed, our hands placed where You want them, and our hearts made new. Reveal our sin so that we may bring it to the foot of the cross and turn from our ways making us more like You. In Jesus' name, Amen.

A Letter To The person Who Is In The Waiting

When will this end? When will this break? Questions like this run through your head day after day, night after night. Maybe you're anxious, doubtful, even angry. If God is real, if He really cares, why can't I feel Him? Why hasn't He come to my rescue yet? The wait feels so long. Too long.

I've been there. I know and have felt all the emotions that waiting brings. It's not easy and it's definitely not pretty, but the lessons I learned in those seasons were only ones that could have been taught in my waiting. Because God uses waiting to change us. He uses it to teach us to rely on Him, to trust Him and to help grow our faith in who He is as a kind, caring, and loving Father. Waiting feels like *something big,* and *nothing* is happening, all at the exact same time.

You know, some of the most prominent people in the Bible were taught what waiting looked like: Abraham, Joseph, Moses, and David, each waited for years, even decades for God's promises to come to fulfillment. If you read each of their stories of endurance, you'll notice that everything that happened during their waiting was used to prepare them inwardly and outwardly for the blessing that was ahead of them. This is exactly what God is doing in *your* heart and life as He prepares you for what's to come.

Please, don't grow weary, my friend. Don't push God aside. Continue to put your hope in who He is. The wait doesn't feel good, but I promise it's worth it because God is always on time, never late. As He grows you and deepens your understanding of who He is through your waiting, trust that He's bringing you to new places in order to receive your breakthrough. Then, when the things you've been praying for begin to fall into place, your character will be ready to handle it.

"But those who hope in the Lord will renew their strength. They will soar on wings like eagles; they will run and not grow weary, they will walk and not be faint." Isaiah 40:31 (NIV). I've loved this verse for as long as I can remember. It's been one that has carried me through many seasons of waiting, and I hope it carries you through your season too. Continue to lean on Jesus, He is your strength and He is with you in your waiting.

Love,

Brooke
xo

Sing like Never Before

"SING PRAISES TO GOD, SING PRAISES; SING PRAISES TO OUR KING, SING PRAISES."

PSALM 47:6 (NIV)

It was during one of my hometown concerts where I saw something that will forever be ingrained in my heart: her name was Susan. She was a woman I grew up going to church with, and was a very dear friend to my family. I remember the day my mom called to tell me that Susan had just been wickedly diagnosed with terminal cancer. News like that is incredibly crushing. It has a way of making you take a step back, put things into perspective and give thanks for the time God's given you here on earth. When Susan was diagnosed, she was immediately admitted to the hospital with no expectation to ever leave, so her kids were told to fly in for their last visit and final goodbyes. But after a shorter time than expected, the doctors decided to let her out, giving her one year to live. And to my surprise, there she was...in the crowd that night at my show.

I remember this moment like it was yesterday. I was in the middle of leading the song "10,000 Reasons" when I opened my eyes and found Susan amongst the people. Her hands were raised high and she was passionately singing the words, "*And on that day when my strength is failing, the end draws near and my time has come, still my soul will sing Your praise unending... ten thousand years, and then forevermore!*" At that moment, I dropped the mic from my mouth, and let the voices in the room carry out the rest of the song.

And there was Susan, blessing His name like she was *never* diagnosed with terminal cancer and had the rest of her life ahead of her. I could see the delight on her face as she sang; it was like she was standing in heaven face to face with Jesus Himself.

I wish I knew exactly where she went in that moment as she poured out her praise, but really, does it even matter? I was reminded that night that our suffering has the ability to drive us closer to Jesus and that worshipping gives our souls a way to bring praise to God, when in the natural, our physical bodies may not be able to.

Psalm 30:12 (TPT) says, "How could I be silent when it's time to praise you? Now my heart sings out loud, bursting with joy— I will give you thanks forever." Imagine if, regardless of our circumstances or situations, we *sang like never before*, or if what we're walking through pushed us closer to the heart of God rather than away, or if in every trial the only thing we could do in His presence was sing and burst with joy. We have so much to bless His name for: the breath in our lungs, the food on our table and in Susan's case, a year to live.

When I saw Susan worshipping, knowing where she had come from and what she had just been through, I couldn't help but be challenged in my own worship. I pray that you would also be challenged today, remembering Susan the next time you "don't feel like worshiping" or "aren't in the mood". In our sickness and brokenness God is still good, still enthroned and still worthy of our praise. May Susan be an inspiration to us all to "sing like never before…"

TAKEAWAY

Whatever you're facing today, you have a reason to worship. We don't praise the Lord of heaven and earth because of all the *things* in our life, but rather because of *who* God is in our life. Write down who you know God to be and let the truth of His character bring hope to your heart reminding you that you too, have a reason to worship.

Bless the Lord oh my soul, Worship His Holy Name. Sing like never before, Oh my soul. I'll worship your Holy Name.

10,000 REASONS

[MATT REDMAN]

God Has a Good Plan For My life

"NO EYE HAS SEEN, NO EAR HAS HEARD, AND NO MIND HAS IMAGINED WHAT GOD HAS PREPARED FOR THOSE WHO LOVE HIM."

1 CORINTHIANS 2:9 (NLT)

I met Eddie at one of my shows a couple years ago. *He was a hard man to miss: tall and wobbly with tubes in his nose and an oxygen tank by his side.* We had a small interaction at my merch table then went our separate ways. But the impact of his kindness and bright white smile followed me as I travelled from city to city.

After meeting Eddie I learned a little bit about his story. He had a significant job at a big company here in Canada, when out of nowhere, he began having what appeared to be mini strokes... or so the doctors thought. In fact, they haven't been able to figure out what's been going on since it all started three years ago. First his eyesight went, then his speech, then his breathing, then the movement of his legs which went on to take his job, home and independence. I can't begin to imagine the reality of such deep loss or how he must feel when he lays his head down at night. Does he wonder "why me?" Does he cry? Does he question who God is? Does he feel scared?

Well, back in the summer, I had the honour of sitting with Eddie at lunch. We ate cheeseburgers and talked about many things, but mostly he encouraged me... go figure. He spoke into my marriage and ministry, telling me how much of a gift I am to him– to which I thought, "oh Eddie, if you only knew the gift you are to me!" At the end of our lunch, he turned with a smile on his face and through a thick stutter said, "God has a *good* plan for my life." Tears filled my eyes, and I was left speechless as we parted ways once again.

It's crazy how some of the most valuable and precious lessons in life are found in the most unpredictable moments. Among others, I'm left with so many questions around Eddie's illness, questions that truthfully may never be answered on this side of heaven. Jeremiah 29:11 (NIV) says, "For I know the plans I have for you," declares the Lord, "plans to prosper you and not to harm you, plans to give you hope and a future." Now, I know this verse can easily be taken out of context because it was meant for the Israelites who had been held in exile for 70 years. God had made this promise to them but the truth is, some didn't even live long enough to see it fulfilled. In some ways, there's a likeness between Eddie and the Israelites because he too is in an exile of sorts. And even in this suffering he's clinging to the hope and peace that God has promised him. He's not asking to be released or set free, he's not begging for answers or even his healing. He's simply trusting and believing that God has *good* plans for his life regardless of his current reality.

Eddie's life is a testimony to us all, that even when we're experiencing pain, or unexpected disasters in our lives, we too can look to the Father and know that He offers us hope, peace and joy in our exile. Sometimes it's easy to get caught up in the things we're walking through and forget that God really does have good plans for our lives. The Bible says that, "No eye has seen, no ear has heard, and no mind has imagined what God has prepared for those who love him." (1 Corinthians 2:9) Rest in the truth of knowing that He has a good plan for you, offering peace and hope through whatever it is you're facing today.

TAKEAWAY
What are you walking through? What is your "exile"? I'm sure we could all take a page out of Eddie's book and *rest* in the unknown, trusting what the word of God promises: peace, hope, joy and comfort. God sees you in your "exile" and He loves you more than you could ever comprehend. His plans for you are GOOD. Speak that over your life today and let the peace of Christ dwell in your heart.

Pass The Coffee!

"SMILE ON ME, YOUR SERVANT. LET YOUR UNDYING LOVE AND GLORIOUS GRACE SAVE ME..."

PSALM 31:16 (TPT)

I was in such a deep sleep that when the jarring sound of my ringtone went off, it startled me so badly that my whole body jolted to a panicked, "I'm awake!" You would have thought somebody yelled "FIRE!" by the way I bolted up, ha! But apparently I didn't mean it, because in my dazed and confused state, I reached over and hit snooze...then I hit snooze again, and again, and one more time until I realized my ride was arriving in 15 minutes. The last time something like this happened to me was in my early twenties, I ignored my alarm with a million snoozes which caused me to almost lose my job. Let's just say it wasn't my best morning, and I had seen better days.

That morning, I felt what I could only describe as deep exhaustion. For whatever the reason, there never seems to be enough hours in the day; at least that seems to be a pretty normal feeling for most of us these days. Some of us have little children, demanding jobs, mouths to feed, houses to clean, dreams to fulfil— the list goes on. There are many verses in the Bible that I could use today, verses that speak to weariness and finding rest in the Lord but Psalm 31:16-17 really stuck out to me. In this verse David is asking the Lord to cut him a break and says, "smile on me, your servant. Let your undying love and glorious grace save me from all this gloom. As I call upon you, let my shame and disgrace be replaced by your favour once again..." I don't know if you can relate, but the more I think about this, I feel a lot like David as He calls out to God for help. Whether you're feeling emotionally worn out, deeply exhausted, or burnt out from the weight and realities of life, God hears you as you cry out for Him to smile upon you and save you from your "gloom".

I'm reminded that in Jesus, there is a rest and a rescue far deeper than any morning coffee or extra sleep has to offer. Nothing will satisfy our cries and our needs like Him, so when we ask God for the things we need, we can guarantee that He'll meet us in our need because that's who He is. When you're feeling worn out by the weight of your reality, ask the Lord to replace your weariness with His strength. And when that deep exhaustion hits, sure– grab a coffee (or if you're like me, a couple!) and ask the Lord to smile upon you as He lavishes His undying love and glorious grace upon you.

There's so much hope to be found in knowing that God hears every cry of our heart, and nothing we whisper or offer unto the Lord goes unheard or missed. At the end of David's prayer he says, "praise be to the Lord, for He showed me the wonders of his love... yet, you heard my cry for mercy when I called to you for help... The Lord preserves those who are true to him... Be strong and take heart, all you who hope in the Lord". (v. 21-24 NIV) Amen, amen and amen! God takes care of all who stay close to Him and just as He answered David's prayer for rescue, He too, will answer yours. Continue to be strong and hope in the Lord to come to your rescue in every area of your life today!

TAKEAWAY

The Bible tells us that the key(s) to finding our rescue is to trust God, serve Him, depend upon Him and realize that "those who wait on the Lord shall renew their strength." (Isa. 40:31 NKJV) So, wherever you feel like you need Jesus to come and give you "deep rest" and rescue today, cry out to Him asking Him to meet you there; He'll hear your cry for mercy and will come to your side with the hope and healing your soul needs.

Come and Rest

"MY PRESENCE WILL GO WITH YOU AND I WILL GIVE YOU REST."

EXODUS 33:14 (ESV)

Rest. Do we even know what that word means anymore? Our culture is busier than ever before and we're bombarded by all that surrounds us as we try to "keep up" with the Joneses. I'm tired just thinking about it!

I came off of a big tour just a few months ago. I was home for *one* day only to pack up, turn around, and head back out for a couple of back-to-back conferences. I did the math of how many hours I had slept that month, and let's just say, it wasn't nearly enough and I was feeling it. Then, I counted the amount of people I had met and interacted with during that time and it was in the thousands! Not to mention, the number of shows I had poured myself into spiritually, emotionally, physically, and mentally. Please don't get me wrong, I'm not complaining and I wouldn't change what I do for anything, but if I had to guess what being on the brink of burnout feels like, it was how I was feeling in that season: totally exhausted and in need of rest. Truthfully, it wasn't a healthy place to be in.

Why does rest feel like some sort of reward these days? Why have we forgotten that rest is not only a commandment but a very precious gift from God? Matthew 11:28 (NIV) says, "Come to me, all you who are weary and burdened, and I will give you rest." God isn't telling us to turn to Him for rest only when we're in the midst of chaos; He wants us to live, to love, to work and to serve from... are you ready for this? A PLACE OF REST. And since God is the giver of rest, we should rest before all else, operating from this place at all times. Trust me, I understand that this sounds backwards in a world that tells us to hustle, hurry up and take on more things, but the way of our God is *not* the way of this world. The Bible says that when we abide in Christ, we will have all we need... we aren't capable of having *all that we need* on our own strength. The word 'abide' means 'to dwell in' or 'live with'; we experience rest when we remain in/dwell in His presence.

Now let's not confuse resting with laziness. To rest in God doesn't mean just laying around doing nothing. Rather, when our *'doing' and 'our being' emerge* from a place of rest, we are then actively believing with faith and living from a place of grace. (And) When faith and grace collide, joy is found and when joy is found, anxiety, fear and burnout run for the hills!

This is rest.

I think we can all agree that we live our best lives, do our best work, love well, and serve more intentionally when we do all these things from a place of rest rather than exhaustion. (Preaching to the choir over here!)

Now, I want to be careful we don't fall into the trap of thinking that rest is a sign of weakness, because it's actually the opposite. When self control and obedience become a part of our daily route, this is faith in action. So, if you're wondering where to start (other than with an obvious nap), choose to carve out time with God. Practice self control by finding solitude and quieting your heart and mind, allowing the Spirit of God to refuel you. I pray that you would learn to live from a place of rest, rather than rest from all your work. Know that God puts these commandments of rest in our lives for our own good. Rest is a gift to both you and I, and I pray that your heart, body, soul and mind would receive it today.

TAKEAWAY

I encourage you to find a quiet place of solitude to spend a few minutes in. Close your eyes and receive His love, joy and peace.

Know that these words are not just feelings, rather, a state of being. Ask the Lord to reveal to you where and how you may need to rest. Slow down. Take a breath. The goal here isn't to be in a rush, living from a place of anxiety and exhaustion. He is with you right now, so shift your heart to the place of His presence today, finding your rest in Him alone.

The Darkness Doesn't Scare Me

"I WILL GO BEFORE YOU AND MAKE THE ROUGH
PLACES SMOOTH…"

ISAIAH 45:2 (NASB)

Imagine sitting at your desk one afternoon when your spouse walks through the door home from work, and out of nowhere says, "I think I need to quit my job."

Welcome to my world. I'm glad you're here...

I remember in that moment wondering if I had heard correctly. It was that feeling of, "I think I heard that right, but I'm really hoping I didn't." (ha!) So I responded with, "I'm sorry, what did you say?" But alas, I had heard him correctly.

Honestly, I didn't want Steve to quit his job. I was working minimally at the church and had just begun touring here and there. I felt really torn between my fear of Steve quitting his job versus what I knew God was leading us to do. How will we eat? How will we pay our rent? This all felt crazy and unreasonable. It felt like I was walking through a thick fog unable to see beyond my current step and God kept asking, "DO YOU TRUST ME?"

During this time, God was really teaching us what it looked like to trust Him. He was calling us both into full time ministry and although He was holding our 'promise' in the palm of his hand, He wasn't giving us a very clear picture of it. We all know it's easy to jump head first into things when we can see the reward in it or at least see what's ahead of us. But it's not so easy when we can't even see what our next step is or where our next meal will come from.

Deuteronomy 31:8 (NIV) says, "The Lord himself goes before you and will be with you; he will never leave you nor forsake you. Do not be afraid..."

I'd be lying if I said my initial reaction was "YES, I TRUST YOU LORD! LET'S DO THIS!" But truthfully, I struggled with trusting Him in this area. Stepping out in faith with your finances and dreams really takes your trust in God to a new level. Some days trusting Him came easily. Other days, I would be clinging to the promise of His Word because I was scared, and I needed to know that He was close.

This is when I began to pray, "I'm not afraid of the darkness..." The Bible promises us that God goes before us in all things, and I'm reminded that the reward in being obedient is far greater than when we choose to do things in our own strength and timing. Even when it's hard and doesn't seem logical... When God calls, we must obey.

So here we are today, standing on the other side of obedience. Our trust has grown, our faith has increased and we've seen God provide time and time again. We know God as a faithful Father in a whole new way, and through many challenges, we've seen Him "carve a path through the pounding waves..." I pray you would lean into the truth of who God is, as "the One who goes before you", knowing that when He calls you out into the waves, He will guide you in His peace and be with you, keeping your head above water. Rest in His many promises today.

TAKEAWAY

Head to wherever it is you listen to music online and play the song, "The Darkness Doesn't Scare Me". Let this song become a declaration for your life, knowing that although you can't always see what's ahead of you, you can be confident in knowing that God goes before you and will lead the way. No matter what darkness or unknown is ahead of you today, go forward in faith knowing *who* goes before you.

I am never afraid. the darkness doesn't scare me. you lead the way, I will stand and be brave. I'm chosen by you father, you call me by name.

THE DARKNESS DOESN'T SCARE ME

[BROOKE NICHOLLS]

I Choose Kindness

"LET LOVE AND KINDNESS BE THE MOTIVATION
BEHIND ALL THAT YOU DO."

1 CORINTHIANS 16:14 (TPT)

I woke up nervous, excited and full of anticipation. I was heading to a stunning studio, east of the city to record my second album. That morning I sent text messages to my pastors and the prayer warriors in my life asking them to pray for me, over the studio, and for anointed worship to flow out of the team and I as we recorded.

My husband got to the studio earlier than me that morning, and as I was pulling into the parking lot, I noticed another familiar car beside his. A few friends quickly crossed my mind but then I didn't think much of it as I put my car in park and frantically gathered my things. I walked through the doors only to be greeted by my girlfriend and her little daughter who had been waiting for me, holding out pink tulips with a note that said, *"Cheering you on, we love you so much."*

You know that feeling when somebody asks how you're doing on a day that you're not doing so well, and you immediately burst into tears? I felt like that, but the opposite. I was so happy that morning knowing somebody saw me, felt my joy, and wanted to join in on my special day. *Cue all the tears of joy!* Who knew that such a small act of kindness could move me so much? I was reminded that we too, can show up with a $10 handful of tulips and make somebody's day. Kindness doesn't have to be grand or expensive. Sometimes it's most moving when shown in small acts like holding the door open, allowing the car in front of us to go first, buying a coffee for somebody, and sometimes it's simply just showing up with flowers in hand. My girlfriend showing up unannounced on one of the most significant days in that season, touched my heart more than she anticipated and it pointed me straight to Jesus, reminding me of His love for me on that day.

Ephesians 4:32 (ESV) says, "be kind to one another, tenderhearted, forgiving one another, as God in Christ forgave you." Kindness is a visible action. Sometimes we have to **choose to be kind** to those we don't feel are deserving, and other times it comes easily. Either way, when we choose kindness, we are choosing Jesus. Kindness is demonstrated throughout Scripture, and by the Holy Spirit, we too can show it the same way Jesus did. By showing kindness, we point people to Him. After all, isn't that what it's all about?

1 Corinthians 16:14 says, *"Let love and kindness be the motivation behind all that you do."* Cultivating the type of kindness that is supernaturally considerate and generous comes from leaning into the teachings and life of Jesus, allowing Him to transform our hearts to be more like Him. Jesus is the best example of what kindness looks like; may we continually become more like Him each and every day.

TAKEAWAY

The Gospels (Matthew, Mark, Luke and John) record Jesus' ministry and show us a lot about who Jesus is and His nature. I encourage you to read through these books of the Bible and take note of the ways Jesus demonstrates kindness to others. He showed kindness without any expectation or agenda. Perhaps there are ways you can show this same kindness to those around you in the days ahead.

I'm Sticking with God

"GOD'S LOYAL LOVE COULDN'T HAVE RUN OUT, HIS MERCIFUL LOVE COULDN'T HAVE DRIED UP. THEY'RE CREATED NEW EVERY MORNING. HOW GREAT IS YOUR FAITHFULNESS! I'M STICKING WITH GOD (I SAY IT OVER AND OVER). HE'S ALL I'VE GOT LEFT."

LAMENTATIONS 3:22 (MSG)

A few summers ago, my husband Steve and I packed up our minivan and drove down to Nashville, Tennessee. We were pinching ourselves the entire ride down because we couldn't believe God had opened the door to such an incredible opportunity: Recording a new record with big producers in the greatest city of all time. And believe it or not, even with this grand adventure at our fingertips, I was still questioning God's plans for my life.

This was an exciting and also very expensive trip. We took what we had been saving for the downpayment of a house, and decided to invest it into what we thought would be a career-breaking opportunity. We arrived in Nashville, and within 24 hours, I started to feel vocally fatigued. We found ourselves in the studio of our dreams, trying to lay vocals over and over, but my voice just wouldn't cooperate. We drove back to Toronto after that week ended feeling so discouraged. Why would God open the door to something so awesome, then make it so discouraging for us? We didn't leave Nashville with magical memories like we had expected, let alone, a new record in hand.

Six months later, we were still facing one road block after another; not only did my voice remain weak and strained for months, but my husband was carrying the weight of working a full time job that he felt God was calling him out of. The first problem with that was that we had just used all our money on the trip to Nashville months before, so we needed him to keep working. The second problem was, it looked like he was going to have a nervous breakdown if he stayed in his job. Let me tell you, it was mayhem in our hearts and household.

I've come to learn that life is hard and comes with *many* questions along the way. One thing I know to be true is that every day I have a God who knows my situations better than I do, and even in my doubts and questions, unrelentingly loves me through them. His mercies are new every morning; God's love is unwavering even in the midst of what feels like disappointment after disappointment. And His love doesn't change according to our circumstances; so when bad things happen and life knocks us down, it doesn't mean God loves us any less. *His love is steadfast* and like a warm extended hand, He invites us to get back up time and time again.

The end of this verse in Lamentations really resonates with me, it says, "I'm sticking with God (I say it over and over). He's all I've got." The truth is, God really is all we've got. When life knocks us down, God's love for us is like a warm extended hand, inviting us to get back up time and time again.

Maybe you've found yourself at a crossroads and were met with disappointment and failed expectations like we were in Nashville. Looking back, it has become so evident that God's hand was all over our situation and was carrying us through that time; of course when you're in the middle of it, it's hard to recognize that truth. I want to remind you today that He's doing the same for you– His loyal love is meeting you exactly where you are, and His faithfulness will see you through all of life's circumstances. So stick with God. He'll see you through it, just like the Bible promises.

TAKEAWAY
Document all of the 'doors' in your life right now that have either been open or closed, then pray over each of them. Perhaps it's job opportunities, friendships or dreams. Whether these are

closed or open doors, ask God for peace around them, for understanding, for a softened heart, and for His plan to unfold for your life. Pray these things for however long feels right– then return to the place you documented everything and write what God has shown you about them since. This will make room for your understanding to be increased and your focus to be more on what He says than how things appear. Remember, God sees the bigger picture of your life and is meeting you with His love, new mercies and faithfulness each and every new day.

Eyes Turned to Jesus

"BUT BLESSED IS THE ONE WHO TRUSTS IN THE LORD, WHOSE CONFIDENCE IS IN HIM."

JEREMIAH 17:7 (NIV)

Between the stresses of work, a crazy travel schedule, maintaining relationships, balancing my marriage and constantly being stretched by what obedience looks like in my ministry, I find myself having to choose to put my trust in who God is daily, drawing my strength from Him alone. Because one day, life looks magical, and the next, I'm broken-hearted over an unravelling dream. Things happen. Sometimes they're discouraging and sometimes they're not. I can try my best but at the end of the day, I don't have control over everything that I do. Jeremiah 17:5-7 says:

"Cursed is the one who trusts in man, who draws strength from mere flesh and whose heart turns away from the LORD. That person will be like a bush in the wastelands; they will not see prosperity when it comes. They will dwell in the parched places of the desert, in a salt land where no one lives. *But blessed is the one who trusts in the LORD, whose confidence is in him."*

Now, "salt land" is a metaphorical name for a desolate no man's land. Basically, I hope nobody finds me in a salt land where no one lives because the Lord knows the extrovert in me would *not* survive! But I really love the picture that this verse paints because it's such a great reminder for us to not draw strength from *anything* other than Jesus. When things in life unexpectedly happen and seasons feel overwhelming, the Bible tells us to put our confidence in the Lord, *trusting in Him alone*—not in the things of this world. We'll never make it out alive if we draw our strength from the world and all that it offers. It's easy to turn to earthly things in our time of need, grasping onto things that we think will instantly soothe the desires of our hearts and minds, but nothing will soothe or comfort us like Jesus.

God always gives us the strength we need to get through things, doesn't He? I think we can all admit that there have been moments in our lives where we haven't necessarily *felt* God in the thick of the mess but as we waited and kept our hearts set on Him, we soon realized He was there all along. If we take a moment to look back on our lives, we'll see God's imprint all over it, empowering us through every decision that needed making, or every task that needed doing. May your heart be reminded of *those* times– the times where you lifted your eyes and whether you felt God or not, chose to put your confidence in who He is.

Perhaps you are in dire need of some God-given strength today and this is resonating with you. Wherever you are, I hope you're encouraged to turn your eyes to Jesus: the giver of life, healer of the heart, the One who sets the captives free, and the One comes to our rescue. Rest in His presence, knowing that nothing in this world can equip you like Jesus can. He was with you then, He is with you now and He'll be with you in the days ahead; keep your eyes on Him.

TAKEAWAY

Maybe you've heard the saying, "you are who you walk with". I believe that this applies to our relationship with Jesus, and that the more time we spend walking with him, the more we become like Him. When we turn our eyes to Jesus, our perspective changes and we're able to face difficulties with a renewed strength. Today, I encourage you to check in with yourself: Are you spending time with Jesus? Are you turning your eyes to Him in all circumstances? Are you drawing your strength from Him? I pray that you would lean on Jesus and not the things of this world, turning your eyes to Him, knowing that He is where your confidence is found.

Pursue

"HOW CAN A YOUNG PERSON LIVE A CLEAN LIFE?
BY CAREFULLY READING THE MAP OF YOUR
WORD. I'M SINGLE-MINDED IN PURSUIT OF YOU;
DON'T LET ME MISS THE ROAD SIGNS
YOU'VE POSTED."

PSALM 119:9-10 (MSG)

I've spent the last few years diving into Psalm 119, which just so happens to be the longest psalm and chapter in the *entire* Bible. Which, by the way, I *did not know* before I decided to dissect it (ha!) I learned that this particular psalm is a hymn of praise and appreciation for God's instructions for our lives. It reminds us that those who follow closely to Him will be filled with joy because God's way is the right way. What would we do as Christians if we didn't have this blueprint directing our steps? But seriously, what *would* we do?

It wasn't that long ago that I met face to face with Jesus in a way that I had never experienced before. I thought I had known Jesus from a young age, but that's what growing up as a Christian can make you believe. Then boom, one day you're on your face weeping at the feet of Jesus realizing that you never really *knew* Him like you thought you did. This obviously isn't everybody's experience, but it certainly was mine.

This specific encounter with Jesus radically changed the way I lived. It opened my eyes to the wonder of who God is, putting the desire in my heart to be in a *single-minded pursuit* of Him. Okay, now you're probably wondering what that even means. Basically, I gave up a job, certain friends and many habits in order to know Jesus on a deep and personal level. And then, the inevitable happened: I began to hear His voice. The closer that I got to Him, the clearer it became.

I have to admit, it was the hardest thing I ever had to do, because I had to give up a lot of things that I didn't necessarily want to give up. But on the other side of that obedience was a great multitude of rewards that were showing me how God was working in things that felt stagnant and dead in my heart. As I kept my eyes open

73

not to miss the road signs that God was posting in front of me, I began to see and understand that He was leading me to the place that He had so desperately wanted to take to me for years. Here's the thing about walking with Jesus– He's always ready and willing to take us to great places. But we need to *choose* to walk with Him first, choosing to lay down everything in our lives, making Him the centre of everything we do.

Verse 10 says, "don't let me miss the road signs you've posted." What imagery! Makes me wonder: Who and what were the road signs that God put in my life that I ignored all those years? When we miss the road signs along the way or stray from where God is leading us, we can cause destruction to our lives; when we are obedient and open to where He wants to take us, the Bible tells us that joy will be our outcome. God's way is the right way and His ways are much higher than ours. It's crazy to think that once upon a time I was blindly walking through life pursuing the things I wanted, ignoring every sign that God was putting in front of me. Have you been there before? It's okay if your answer is yes– I think it's safe to say most of us have been (or still are) there.

But here's the good news, you can open your heart and make the decision to be in a *single-minded pursuit* of Jesus today. It might not be the easiest thing you do, but it'll be the most worthwhile decision you'll ever make. He is worthy of your time, your decision making, your conversations and your actions. Rest in the truth of knowing that when you pursue God in *all* areas of your life, not just the ones you want, He leads you to a path of hope, of living water and a place of abundant joy.

TAKEAWAY

Ask yourself these questions and answer them as honestly as you can:

- Have I been missing God's road signs?
- Do I feel God calling me to give up things that are hindering me from pursuing Him?
- Am I in a single-minded pursuit of Him and Him alone? If not, how come?

It's never too late to begin the journey with Jesus. Whether you've been a Christian your whole life like me or this is a new concept for you, His mercies are new every day, and every moment is a moment to surrender your life fully to Him!

I'm praying for you today.

I pursue you God. Chase after your promises. Pursue your heart and the pattern of your ways.

PURSUE

[BROOKE NICHOLLS]

Forget The Old

"FORGET THE FORMER THINGS; DO NOT DWELL ON THE PAST."

ISAIAH 43:18 (NIV)

Let's face it, we've all done things in our life that we wish we could erase and forget about. Unfortunately, that's just not how life works, but thanks be to God who lovingly offers us freedom from guilt and shame and new life through Jesus. (And everybody shouts "AMEN!")

When we stay focused on our past, we miss what God is doing in our now. Let that sink in for a moment: God is doing something in your "now." And as God is calling us out into new territory, it's easy to find ourselves looking more at our limitations or our past, rather than at His great power and freedom. I can't even count the number of times I've sat down at the piano to write a song only to sit in silence experiencing total writer's block; which made me question my ability to sing, write and record albums. Don't even get me started on how many days I woke up telling myself, "I don't have the gift of writing because of my past grades– I guess I have no business writing a devotional." And my favourite lie, "God could never use somebody like you with a past like yours." Umm, wrong! God doesn't want us to miss out on the things He's calling us to because we're continually looking behind us believing all sorts of lies from the enemy. Instead, He desperately wants to realign our hearts so that we're not held back from moving on into the new things that He has in store for us.

It's so easy to see all the ways we've fallen short and failed in the past and if you're anything like me, I tend to count my shortcomings first (like radio silence on writing days, bad grades in high school, and past mistakes) *long* before I consider my strengths. I'm thankful and challenged by the beginning of this verse found in Isaiah and I hope you are too. It simply says, "Forget the former things." With our eyes fixed on our past, we can't see the way forward, but with our eyes fixed on Jesus and his forgiving heart, we actually allow God to move and unfold the new thing He has prepared for us. I don't know about you, but I desperately want *that* for my life! Imagine if we all just listened to the lies of our past? Thank you Jesus for your grace and freedom!

What do you need to allow yourself to be forgiven for so that you can move forward into the calling God has on your life? Be encouraged today knowing that God does not condemn you for your past but is instead holding out His hand of hope and giving you an opportunity to enter into a new thing! Don't let the shadows of your past keep you imprisoned. Don't be afraid to step into the newness that God is calling you into. I'm praying for you today as God exchanges your past for His hope-filled future.

TAKEAWAY

Grab a journal. Sometimes the good ol' pen to paper is a good way to slow down and hear what God wants to say to you. What's the dream in your heart? Is there something from your past keeping you from that dream? Is there something that is reminding you of all the ways you once failed or let people down? Write it down and exchange those lies and guilt for God's truth and forgiveness. This will bring freedom to your heart in a way that only God can bring.

A Sacrificial love

"WITH TENDER HUMILITY AND QUIET PATIENCE,
ALWAYS DEMONSTRATE GENTLENESS AND
GENEROUS LOVE TOWARD ONE ANOTHER..."

EPHESIANS 4:2 (TPT)

I've been married for a number of years and was recently challenged to step back and take a look at my marriage. My husband makes loving him extremely easy, but I didn't know what loving sacrificially actually looked like, until I got married. And since that beautiful August 7th day, God has been teaching me what loving without limits *can* look like. I've realized that it's easy to think that only "other people" get divorced and that your own marriage is somehow immune to heartache. But the truth is: Marriage is hard work and it's expressed in a lot of different ways. It's a simple coffee on an extra sleepy morning, practicing being slow to speak in a heated moment, or understanding that my need or want might not be the top priority that day. I'm not ashamed to say that I work hard to try and love Steve well. I think it's important for people to know that with Christ, marriage can be the most delightful, joyful adventure in the world.

Please don't misunderstand what I'm saying. It has taken years of mistakes and painful falls to learn this kind of love. Through God's word, I'm still learning, still healing, and still trying my best. This verse from Ephesians 4:2 says, "With tender humility and quiet patience, always demonstrate gentleness and generous love toward one another..." I won't lie, the call to love my husband in this way isn't an easy one, but with prayer (lots of it) and help from the Holy Spirit, I try to posture my heart everyday to be generous with this kind of love. Now, quiet patience on the other hand... that's a different story, ha!

No marriage is perfect, but it sure can be wonderful. We don't always get it right, but with Christ leading the way, we're always forgiven. Marriage isn't about you and your happiness, but rather about living a life of holiness and sacrificial love, doing your best to point each other to Jesus. And even as I sit here typing this truth out, I feel a deep conviction around holiness and sacrificial love vs. my selfish need to always want to feel happy.

Marriages need all the support and prayers they can get (can I get an amen?). So let's be there for each other! May you run the race well on this side of heaven with more endurance, spurring one another on towards Christ in deeper ways. God loves you and your spouse and He shows up in things like our marriages when we submit our lives and all that they include fully to Him.

TAKEAWAY

Take time to go and pray with your spouse. Hand in hand, invite the Holy Spirit in and then ask for forgiveness from one another in areas you may have fallen short. Together, pray for your marriage as you feel led to, practicing the words found in Ephesians 4:2 and remember to have grace for one another. Ask God to show you the areas of your heart that He is currently shaping and be encouraged knowing that the same hands that created the universe are the same ones holding both your heart's today.

To The person Who Doesn't Feel Enough

It's 6:30 AM, your alarm goes off and you roll over to grab your phone. You scroll...and scroll...and scroll some more, becoming inundated with other people's lives and essentially, what is considered as their 'highlight reel.' You feel overwhelmed by all their 'success', beauty, picture-perfect homes, and relationships. You look and can't help but think, "If only I was *that* beautiful, had those clothes, money and wow, that perfect relationship that reminds me of a Hallmark movie." If only...if only... if only... Your day hasn't even started yet and you've already torn yourself down with a million "if onlys."

My dear reader, who told you that you weren't enough? Who told you that you needed to be 'more' or 'better', and that "if onlys" were acceptable to live by? Listen, I'm not judging you for feeling these things, because I've felt them before too. We all have. But let's just be clear in saying that God certainly didn't tell us these crazy lies. On the days when we don't love ourselves, God actually loves us beyond our ability to comprehend and *nothing will be able to separate us from that love*. God never intended for us to covet other people's lives, rejecting the way we've been created. So the next time you are scrolling, remember that loving ourselves the way God designed us to does not include measuring ourselves against each other.

When we actively remain in God's love, we won't be drawn into the things of this world. No blogger, influencer, ex-girlfriend or boyfriend can steal your joy and the truth of who you are, which is… enough. Your quirks are charming, you are loved for who you are, where you are and exactly as you are; *there is nobody like you*.

So give it all to God, sweet friend. He wants to hold you in your insecurities and feelings of inadequacy. He longs for you to know and believe that you are enough in Him. He made you exactly the way He wanted you to be, so come and rest, knowing that you are enough. You are more, you are chosen, God is for you, with you, you are crowned a son or daughter and God calls you His very own. And hey, some days will be harder than others, and that's okay. Go easy on yourself. Step-by-step, day-by-day. Come on, say this with me… "I am enough."

Love,

Put worry to rest

"CAST YOUR ANXIETY ON THE LORD BECAUSE HE CARES FOR YOU."

1 PETER 5:7 (NIV)

I used to worry about *everything.* I'd worry about the things of the past, things of the future, and things of the present. But I learned quickly (or not so quickly) that nothing can be added to our lives by worrying. Instead, it keeps us up at night, gives us headaches and raises our blood pressure. And I mean, that's just a *few* of the things it does to us physically, not to mention mentally and emotionally.

But 1 Peter 5:7 puts our worrying little hearts at ease and encourages us "to cast our anxiety on the Lord because He cares for us." I'm reminded that Jesus really is the great physician and when we give Him the worries of our day, He draws close and trades them with His supernatural peace. But I know how hard it can be to hold fast to this truth when tough times hit. We end up worrying about the things seen and unseen, remembering the most negative parts of events, and forgetting both the good and the truth. The good news is, there is hope in Jesus, the One who carries our pain and not only that, has the power to heal it. He knows everything there is to know. He knows how afraid we are, how bad we feel, what scares us, and through it all— He remains close, inviting us to cast it all on Him. Our goal should always be to stay faithful to the Word of God, allowing *His* peace to reign in our hearts.

Matthew 6:31-34 (CSB) says, "So don't worry, saying, 'What will we eat?' or 'What will we drink?' or 'What will we wear?' For the Gentiles eagerly seek all these things, and your heavenly Father knows that you need them. But seek first the kingdom of God and his righteousness, and all these things will be provided for you. Therefore don't worry about tomorrow, because tomorrow will worry about itself. Each day has enough trouble of its own."

There it is! Seek His kingdom *first!* Instead of worrying about tomorrow and making yourself sick with anxiety, trust that the Lord cares enough about you to provide the things that you need, exactly when you need them. Take all the things you worry about (family, finances, careers, health, etc.) and give them to God, knowing that the same God who meets you in your joys is the same God who wants to meet you in your worries. He doesn't want you to live a life filled with anxiety that makes you sick. Instead, He wants you to chase after the things of His kingdom. With a heart turned toward Him, you can take comfort in knowing that He wants to restore you, confirm you, strengthen you, and establish you– for His sake and for your good. So, put your worry to rest and leave it in the hands of the One who cares oh so deeply for you. Make today be the day you exchange your worries for God's perfect peace!

TAKEAWAY

I wrote these lyrics in a time where worry felt all consuming– maybe you can relate. As you read the words on the next page out loud, allow them to shift the worry in your heart into a deep trust in who holds your tomorrow and the things in it. Lean in and remember God's promises over your life instead of trying to hold things together in your own strength. Know that God is near, holding you in whatever season you may find yourself in; cast your worries on Him today.

Oh God, You're Near
you're holding me
in every season
and situation
No I won't fear
Refining me through
the fire
your ways are
always higher

YOU'RE NEAR
[BROOKE NICHOLLS]

God Goes Before You

"DO NOT YIELD TO FEAR, FOR I AM ALWAYS
NEAR. NEVER TURN YOUR GAZE FROM ME, FOR I
AM YOUR FAITHFUL GOD. I WILL INFUSE YOU WITH
MY STRENGTH AND HELP YOU IN EVERY
SITUATION. I WILL HOLD YOU FIRMLY WITH MY
VICTORIOUS RIGHT HAND."

ISAIAH 41:10 (TPT)

I woke up earlier than usual one morning from a dream. Totally not the norm for me, because I'm a sleeper who often forgets her dreams, but this day and this dream was different. All I can remember is this: I was walking through a pitch back tunnel, I was filled with confidence and peace when suddenly, failure, sickness, broken dreams and death all flashed before my very eyes. Then, boom...I woke up. What on earth was that all about? Why was I so confident when so many sad things were flashing before me? I sat with the imagery of this dream for over two years as I began to face loss, failure and broken dreams in *my own* life. All of a sudden I felt like my life *became* the dark tunnel from my dream; I couldn't see through to the other side and I had no idea what was ahead of me, yet in my life I had this confidence in who Jesus was and peace as I continued to walk.

In John 14:27 (GNB) the Lord says, "Peace is what I leave with you; it is my own peace that I give you. I do not give it as the world does. Do not be worried and upset; do not be afraid." Peace. How comforting to know that there's a peace unlike any other that we have access to through Jesus. God gives us all we need to confidently go through the things that we don't quite understand or even see to the other side of, and because of that, we don't have to fear the unknown. The plans God has for our lives aren't any less purposeful just because we're walking through them in the dark.

There's a peace that comes from knowing *who God is* when we're scared and have no idea where or when to take our next step. And there's a peace that rests on us in an unexplainable way when we truly understand how God loves us, cares for us and provides for us. Isaiah 41:10 says, "Do not yield to fear, for I am always near. Never turn your gaze from me, for I am your faithful

God. I will infuse you with my strength and help you in every situation." What a promise that God remains close to us in the midst of life's uncertainties or storms. And with our eyes fixed on Him, we don't have to be afraid because He gives us all we need to walk in peace that infuses us with His strength.

Life can be hard, there's no question about that. But as we draw near to God, He reminds us that His word is filled with great hope and many promises to lead us to the other side. I pray that His word would be a lamp unto your feet as you continue to put one foot in front of the other, feeling assured that He is with you in whatever you are facing today. In the turmoil, the struggles, the anxious thoughts and worries of life. He is there strengthening, helping, and holding you in His hands; do not be afraid as His peace and presence lights your dark tunnel.

TAKEAWAY

Peace can be an easy word to throw around in conversation, yet an extremely difficult word to actually feel and live from. The word peace means "freedom from disturbance; tranquility." And as Christians we carry the presence of God with us, which means we also carry peace in our hearts.

I want to encourage you to write down the areas of your life that you need the Lord to infuse with His peace, bringing you freedom knowing that He goes before you. Give these areas to the Lord and pray over each one. Ask God to guard your heart and mind as you trade in fear, doubt and anxiety for His undeniable, unexplainable, perfect peace. Ask Him to empower you to walk in confidence through any unknowns as the peace of Christ reigns in your heart today.

Because Of My Chains

"...WHAT I'M GOING THROUGH HAS ACTUALLY
CAUSED MANY BELIEVERS TO BECOME EVEN
MORE COURAGEOUS IN THE LORD..."

PHILIPPIANS 1:14 (TPT)

A heroin addict, living on the streets willing to do anything for his next fix, turned preacher of the Gospel and husband to my best friend. Okay, say what?

This is the kind of story I had read about in *other* people's books, but had never witnessed it for myself, until now. I've heard many people say that God could never use "someone like me" because of their past. I always laugh under my breath when I hear this because if you know God, then you know He's the king (no pun intended) of taking the dirtiest, most broken and messy lives, and turning them into the most beautiful masterpieces.

When Matt was living on the streets of California, I'm sure he never imagined what his life 15 years down the road would look like: A sober, godly husband expecting a baby boy, leading worship and preaching the good news of Jesus. You know, it's one thing to just *hear* these stories but it's another thing to actually *know* the person; honestly, as I type this I could cry at how amazing God is. I'm reminded that God never let go of Matt's tender heart and although Matt was far from the Lord, the Lord was *never* far from Matt. And before Matt even knew the Lord... the Lord *knew* Matt.

When Paul got thrown into prison for sharing the Gospel, he wrote the book of Philippians. And in it he wrote a letter to the church at Philippi saying, "I want you to know, dear ones, what has happened to me has not hindered, but helped my ministry of preaching the gospel, causing it to expand and spread to many people...And what I'm going through has actually caused many believers to become even more courageous in the Lord and to be bold and passionate to preach the word of God, all because of my chains." (Phil. 1:12,14, TPT)

Although the stories here are different, they feel inescapably similar in some ways. Matt wasn't thrown into prison and Paul wasn't a drug addict, but the parallel looks to be found in the last verse: "*what I'm going through has actually caused many believers to become even more courageous in the Lord and to be bold and passionate to preach the Word of God, all because of my chains*." There it is! *All because of my chains*. Matt's entire life has been redeemed and restored. By the blood of Jesus he has been set free and forgiven, and by the grace of God he is now leading others to accept that same gift. It's because of his chains that he is in the place that he's in today, and it's also because of those chains that others are being radically saved. How incredible that our 'chains' have the ability to be used for God's glory to advance His Kingdom! Be encouraged today in knowing that God can use anybody. Yes, *anybody*! Never doubt where God will lead you; it's *because of your chains* that God can bring you into the darkest places to be a light to the world. I pray that you would find hope in Matt's story, but also hope in knowing that the same God who redeemed and restored Matt's life, is the same God who wants to redeem and restore yours. He wants to take where you've been and use it for His name's sake and glory, in Jesus' name!

TAKEAWAY

Isn't God so good? The things you've done or the places you've gone in your life don't matter— God is redeemer, healer, restorer and He wants to use you today. He wants to use your story to touch the lives of those in your very own home, workplace and those you come into contact with throughout your day. Ask God how He can use your story for His glory, and pray that He would begin to open doors for you to share the good news of His redemptive love with the lost!

worship is a weapon

"I WILL SING TO THE LORD AS LONG AS I LIVE. I WILL PRAISE MY GOD TO MY LAST BREATH!"

PSALM 104:33 (NLT)

It was a late Friday night as I sat at my piano. The street lights from outside lit up my fingers as I played with no specific song in mind. There were, what felt like, a million thoughts running through my head, and although I knew I needed God in that moment, I didn't exactly know *what* that looked like. As I leaned in closer to find some comfort, I heard Him say, "SING." So I did. The words I began to sing didn't rhyme, there was no order to them, and truthfully, they didn't make a whole lot of sense. But those words were from my heart to God's, and in that moment, that's all that really mattered.

Worship is a powerful weapon. It's a weapon that can unlock doors, break chains, bring healing and deliverance, and cause the enemy to back up and take his hands off you. In that moment at my piano I learned that worship really is our weapon, which got me thinking, *why on earth are we ever silent?*

I'm reminded of the story of Paul and Silas found in the book of Acts, two worshippers thrown into jail, making worship their greatest weapon. Acts 16:23-26 (NASB) reads:

"When they had struck them with many blows, they threw them into prison, commanding the jailer to guard them securely; and he, having received such a command, threw them into the inner prison and fastened their feet in the stocks. But about midnight Paul and Silas were praying and singing hymns of praise to God, and the prisoners were listening to them; and suddenly there came a great earthquake, so that the foundations of the prison house were shaken; and immediately all the doors were opened and everyone's chains were unfastened."

I love how God responds to our worship. In this case, He shook the prison to its foundation, removing their chains and setting them free. Just like He did with Paul & Silas, the Holy Spirit enables us to lift up our song during difficult times. We too, have the same power in us to worship this way– a way that causes the "foundation to shake" and the "chains to fall off." The truth is, the enemy wants us to live defeated. He wants you to stay sick and heartbroken. He wants you to feel worthless and cheap and stay imprisoned to guilt and shame. I don't know about you, but that makes me want to worship LOUDER, lifting high my weapon of worship to the *only* God who has the authority and power to set us free! The atmosphere really does shift when we raise our voices and prayers to God. Come on, say it with me: *"If worship is my weapon, then I will not be silent!"*

I hope we can all be like Paul and Silas, worshipping in our darkest hour, shifting the atmosphere, and allowing *who we know God to be* to reign over any worry or anxiety. Psalm 104:33 (NLT) says, "I will sing to the LORD as long as I live. I will praise my God to my last breath!" You don't need to have musical abilities to open your mouth and call out to the Lord. And just like that night at my piano, it doesn't need to have any real formation, because God knows your heart and bends down to hear every song and whispered prayer. May worship be your weapon today!

TAKEAWAY

Worship God in the moments where things feel unknown or fearful. Don't worry about trying to remember or recite your favourite worship song– just sing spontaneously the feelings of your heart, allowing worship to become your greatest weapon. Sing these words over and over again; whether they are momentary or a song for your season, lift them high knowing that God hears them, rejoices in them, and will respond to every one of them.

Then Sings My Soul

"YOU ARE WONDERFUL, LORD, AND YOU DESERVE ALL PRAISE, BECAUSE YOU ARE MUCH GREATER THAN ANYONE CAN UNDERSTAND."

PSALM 145:3 (CEV)

"How Great Thou Art" has been playing on my stereo since I was a little girl. I grew up in a small Pentecostal church, where Sunday worship consisted of a handful of hymns found in the old pages of the hymnals that were tucked in the pew ahead of me. We don't really sing these songs in church like we used to, but I still live for the oldies because the truth that's found in them isn't limited to a specific date in time. They rang true then... and they ring true now.

When I released my first Christian album back in 2016, I had my heart set on adding some of my favourite hymns to it. I think we can all agree that there's just something so special and sacred about a hymn– the way it's written, the truth in every lyric, and the reminder that we are not the first generation who have wrestled, prayed, asked, and believed. I love how music has a way of connecting us to the Father and how every song has a special story behind it, personal and unique to its writer.

A Swedish man named Carl Boberg wrote "How Great Thou Art" in 1885, and as the story goes, he was walking home from church when he was caught in a major thunderstorm. He hurried for shelter as violent flashes of lightning struck and crashes of thunder rang through the sky. When he got home, the storm had settled and he was then met with a beautiful rainbow. We all know the feeling that a rainbow gives us, don't we? I don't know about you but for whatever reason, I want to take a million photos and have that bright and colourful moment last forever. The story goes on to say that as Carl cracked open his window overlooking the sea, listening to the calm sound of the birds singing, he "fell on his knees in humble adoration of his mighty God."

Psalm 145:3 says, "You are wonderful, LORD, and you deserve all the praise, because you are much greater than anyone can understand." I love how this verse tells it like it is. Basically, our human understanding can't even grasp the vastness of God's greatness. Isn't that wild to think about? When I look at the stars, or see rainbows, or waves as they crash, I'm always in awe of God's power and works... but to think, that's just a *mere* glimpse into His greatness. A simple scratch on the surface.

What an awe-inspiring day that must have been for Carl– one that birthed such a powerful and truth-filled hymn. It's true, when we experience something as breathtaking as Carl did, it's hard *not* to respond in worship by falling to our knees declaring how great and mighty God's works are. The beauty of this song turns our eyes to Jesus reminding us that God is greater than any joy this world has to offer, and greater than any storm our souls will ever weather. As I read the lyrics, I am once again reminded that the gospel isn't about me and how I'm doing; rather, it's about our great God and what He's done for us. My prayer is that this hymn would lift your gaze today, reminding you of God's goodness and faithfulness.

TAKEAWAY

Meditate on the lyrics of the hymn on the next page. Find the beauty in every word, letting them fill your heart and soul today. And as you sit in this moment, think about His works, taking time to give God thanks for His awesome wonder! How great is our God!

Then sings my soul, my Savior God to Thee, how great thou art how great thou art

HOW GREAT THOU ART

[CARL BOBERG]

God's Perfect Plan

"A PERSON MAY HAVE MANY IDEAS CONCERNING
GOD'S PLAN FOR HIS LIFE, BUT ONLY THE DESIGNS
OF HIS PURPOSE WILL SUCCEED IN THE END."

PROVERBS 19:21 (TPT)

We all have dreams as we grow up. When I was younger, I wanted to have five kids all named after my family members; there was a Collie dog, a horse and a farm involved. I wanted to be an orthodontist or maybe a model. I'm not sure what TV show I was watching when those two careers made it onto the front page of my diary at the age of 11, but here we are. As I sit to write this, I don't have kids yet, I don't have a dog or a horse, I don't live on a farm and I DEFINITELY didn't become a model.

My dreams changed as I grew older. I didn't want to have kids, I lived in a condo in downtown Toronto, and I was pursuing a life in pop music.

And now, here I am, many years later: praying for children, living in the suburbs and working in full-time ministry. I'm reminded of this verse in Proverbs 19 that says, "many are the plans in the mind of a man but it's the purpose of the Lord that will stand." We all have plans but it's not until we get ourselves into the quiet, still presence of God that we're able to listen and be led by the Holy Spirit. For many years I knew God was calling me into ministry, but I kept myself so busy and distracted, ignoring every person or sign that tried to tell me I was meant for ministry.

It's okay if your dreams have changed. It's okay that the idea of what you once thought could be is no longer. That happens. But what we need to keep sight of is how open-handedly we're holding onto those dreams and allowing God to have His way in our life. Deuteronomy 7:6 (MSG) reminds us that, "God chose you out of all the people here on earth for himself as his personal cherished treasure." I love how even when we are distracted and busy holding our dreams in our tight fists, God doesn't give up on us or stop reminding us of how he loves us and chooses us. I pray you would lean into His love and affection, being reminded that wonderful dreams blossom when we operate from this sacred and intimate place.

Open hands... open heart... Lord, have your way.

It's hard to understand the plans God has for us when we are so inwardly focused. However, when we invite Jesus into our lives and turn our eyes upon Him, we allow Him to speak purpose into our dreams and future. You are unique. Only you can do what God has called you to do. It's easy to compare ourselves and feel jealous of what others are doing with their lives. But I beg you, don't miss out on where God is trying to bring you because your eyes are on others rather than on Jesus. Eyes up and heart open– God wants all your attention today.

TAKEAWAY

Give God all of your dreams. The house, the kids, and in my case, my teenage modelling career (ha!). Give them back to Him with open hands. Let go of your desire to know every outcome, trusting that God's plans for your life are timely and perfect. Take time to sit with Jesus, pushing all distractions aside and pray that God would help you see the areas of your life that you're holding onto that need to be released to Him today. Ask Him where He wants to lead you and how He wants to use you as He unravels His perfect plans for your life.

You are a Priest

"BUT YOU ARE A CHOSEN PEOPLE, A ROYAL PRIESTHOOD, A HOLY NATION, GOD'S SPECIAL POSSESSION, THAT YOU MAY DECLARE THE PRAISES OF HIM WHO CALLED YOU OUT OF DARKNESS INTO HIS WONDERFUL LIGHT."

1 PETER 2:9 (NIV)

I've been attending church for over 30 years and leading worship for over a decade now. This verse in 1 Peter has just recently changed the way I view the local church, the way I worship on and off stage, and the way I lead congregations. It's changed how I see myself in the eyes of God and as a person building the church, because *I am a priest* and guess what? You're a priest too.

Whether you're part of a worship team, a creative team, a tech team or sitting in the pews on a Sunday morning; if you're a believer, God has called you a priest. I don't know about you, but when I hear the word "priest," I think of a man in a white robe standing at the front of a Roman Catholic church, lighting candles, and leading mass with some sort of reading. Culture has really impacted what we think when we hear the word *priest*, hasn't it? But, did you know this was never how God intended it to be? He never intended a ranking system to dominate. He never intended for His priesthood to be restricted to a few people in a certain tribe. He never intended leadership to be limited to those who have fancy titles or high positions of authority in the church. We (man) created that barrier, not God.

Get this: The early Roman Catholic Church (a bajillion years ago) decided that only they could ordain priests, then the rest of the church followed suit. Yet, the Word of God in 1 Peter 2:5 (MSG) says to, "present yourselves as building stones for the construction of a sanctuary vibrant with life, in which you'll serve as holy priests offering Christ-approved lives up to God." This verse isn't just for ordained men serving in the Catholic church– *it's for all of us*! It's for any Christian man or woman who declares that Jesus Christ is their Lord and Saviour because we were all made priests as soon as we gave our lives to Jesus.

Our job as a priest is to worship God and set up meeting places between God and other people. Everywhere we go, we are a priest giving people an opportunity to meet with Jesus. Whether we're at the office, in the lineup at Walmart, or at home with our family, we are... priests! Let that sink in for a moment.

Now, imagine the shift in our churches if we all showed up on a Sunday *ready* to worship as priests. I know we often leave it up to the worship leader to draw us into worship, but as we shift into this priestly mentality, it will allow us to come *ready*. Ready with a heart eager to engage with Jesus, knowing that we too, carry the presence of God and have the authority to lead those around us to an encounter with the Living God. (*Insert revival here*)

I pray God would continue to open the eyes of your heart so that you would walk in authority, knowing that God has ordained and given you the title of a priest to lead generations upon generations to Jesus!

TAKEAWAY

Write the word "priest" on a sticky note and go stick it somewhere (like a mirror, your laptop or desk) to remind yourself that you are a priest and you play a huge role in pointing those around you to Jesus. Ask the Lord what being a priest means to Him and how He wants you to walk in your priesthood. Pray for strength to carry this torch with vibrant life as you continue to surrender your life to Jesus!

Holiness Over Happiness

"...BUT AS HE WHO CALLED YOU IS HOLY, YOU ALSO
BE HOLY IN ALL YOUR CONDUCT, SINCE IT IS
WRITTEN, "YOU SHALL BE HOLY, FOR I AM HOLY."

1 PETER 1:15-16 (ESV)

A few years back I was going through a confusing time in my life. Being the mama's girl that I am, I would call her every day, sometimes twice a day (hey, don't judge!) just to hear her voice. Hearing it brought me comfort. There's something about a mother's voice that brings healing in a time of need. My mom is wise, she walks closely with the Lord and I knew I could count on her to listen without judgment. In every conversation, she would remind me that God was calling me to live a life of holiness and would ask me, "And are you?" The answer to that question was a big fat "no" and if I'm being totally honest, that wasn't the advice I was looking for. I wanted her to tell me to go and live my life, doing whatever I needed to find contentment and happiness. Talk about leaving it up to a mom to say the thing we *actually* need to hear, not the thing we *want* to hear; thanks a lot, Mom.

The word 'holy' means, "to be set apart." Though God wants us to feel happiness, we actually derail when our happiness takes precedence over our holiness. Happiness is based on our emotions and we all know that emotions are fleeting– they come and go like the wind. Instead, holiness is a dedicated act of daily worship; seeking God in all that we do. The good news is, we don't have to choose one over the other, because when we make holiness our priority happiness follows.

It took me years to understand this call to holiness. Through my pursuit of happiness I learned that there is no true happiness apart from holiness and no holiness apart from Christ. I want to be clear in saying that I believe seeking to follow God and seeking happiness can go hand-in-hand, but sadly, we live in a culture that has become so inwardly focused on self-satisfaction, self-fulfilment, and personal happiness that we've started to lose sight of what holiness actually looks like. We've made it all about me, me, me, vs God, God, God.

This verse found in 1 Peter 1:15-16 is a good reminder— or maybe even a wake up call— for some of us. It reads, "...but as He who called you is holy, you also be holy in all your conduct, since it is written, 'You shall be holy, for I am holy.'"

When we're facing decisions about how to live, remember God didn't command us to "be happy for I am happy." No, He said "be holy, for I am holy." The verse goes on to say, "let yourselves be pulled into a way of life shaped by God's life, a life energetic and blazing with holiness." (v. 15, MSG) I want to encourage you to look at the different ways you can begin living a life of holiness: set your heart and mind on the Word, practice self-control, cultivate discipline, and turn from your sin. John Piper states, "It can be very misleading at best to say God desires your obedience more than your happiness, because obedience to these commands is happiness." Let that idea sink in for a minute... how powerful!

Although I wasn't keen on my mom's advice at that confusing time, I'm so thankful she continued to remind me of God's call to holiness in my life. And I pray that as Christians, we wouldn't become immune to sin, chasing happiness at our own expense, but rather, remind one another what it looks like to lay down our life and choose God's way. I'm praying that today, you would know and understand what it looks like to live a life shaped by God's call— a life blazing with holiness!

TAKEAWAY

Ask your heart if you really understand the *true* meaning of holiness. Once you grasp how a life of holiness will lead you closer to Jesus, ask the Holy Spirit to reveal what things you may need to lay down or pick up. What have you been holding onto that has been making you happy, but driving a wedge between you and the Lord? What are some ways you can practice a life of holiness? Remember, living a life of holiness leads to a life of happiness, not the other way around.

He who Has promised is Faithful

"LET US HOLD UNSWERVINGLY TO THE HOPE WE PROFESS, FOR HE WHO PROMISED IS FAITHFUL."

HEBREWS 10:23 (NIV)

My husband and I were recently house hunting, and truthfully, I had no idea what I was getting myself into. I was feeling every emotion possible during this process and let me tell you, it wasn't pretty.

One day I'd be dreaming of having a quiet, serene space to be still and create in, then the next day I'd get a phone call telling me we had no chance of purchasing in the current market. I was picturing a home like I grew up in, one to raise a family in and make memories in. Then, low and behold I'd open my emails only to find houses with missing roofs and broken staircases with captions that read: "RARE FIND FOR FIRST TIME HOME BUYERS." Yeah… rare find is right.

I love this verse in Hebrews 10 that says, "He who has promised is faithful." Short and simple, yet hopeful. What a reminder that in any stressful or uncertain season, we need to trust the process. Why? Because God is faithful. The promise of God's unfailing presence is what matters most, which enables us to walk in confidence and contentment. No matter how many disappointments or unfulfilled promises we experience in life (or in our case, broken house dreams), God's presence follows us and His promised faithfulness prevails. And here's the honest truth: it may not look like what you had envisioned. But whatever the outcome, we need to be reminded that His promises are upheld by His flawless character, which includes being: faithful, just, loving, eternal, righteous, sovereign and truthful (just to name a few!).

So, in times when we don't understand the process, we need to remind ourselves that God's feelings for us don't change. He is a trustworthy Father and His character remains true in our time of uncertainty. Therefore: We *need* to trust Him and keep our hearts set on His mighty works. When we keep our eyes on the 'prize' it helps shift our hearts and minds from earthly to heavenly, giving us eternal perspective. In saying that, my tiny house sure is cute, but am I ever looking forward to that mansion in heaven! Ha! Perhaps this is a pep talk for my own heart, or perhaps God has placed this word on my heart today to help point you to Him. Turning to Jesus isn't like a lamp that you rub to make a genie appear in hopes that all your wishes come true. Instead, turning to Jesus gives us peace and perspective in a discouraging process or season, which increases our faith and builds our trust in who God is. Do not lose hope. God is with you in all that you're facing, and... He who has promised is faithful.

TAKEAWAY

What are you facing that feels overwhelming or discouraging? What are you hoping and believing for in your life or in the life of your family?

Let the words to the song "Never Once" by Matt Redman remind your heart that never once has the Lord left you to fight or figure things out on our own. Rest in His presence knowing that He promises to be faithful and see you through.

Never Once did we ever walk alone. Never Once did you leave us on our own. You are faithful, God, you are faithful.

NEVER ONCE

[MATT REDMAN]

I Choose Forgiveness

"GET RID OF ALL BITTERNESS, RAGE AND ANGER, BRAWLING AND SLANDER, ALONG WITH EVERY FORM OF MALICE [...] FORGIVE EACH OTHER, JUST AS IN CHRIST GOD FORGAVE YOU."

EPHESIANS 4:31-32 (NIV)

I sat in a circle with some friends talking about forgiveness and dissecting the acute importance of it. The 'why' behind needing to forgive people who hurt us when we were kids, teenagers, and even today as adults was something we were all being uncomfortably confronted with as we sat around the table together.

We challenged each other to ask the Lord to reveal who had hurt us over the years. Who said something that felt unforgivable? Who rejected us? Who went behind our back? Who gossiped about us? Who deliberately hurt our feelings? Who have we consciously or subconsciously been holding ransom in our hearts? I would be lying if I said nobody came to mind, but in that moment I was faced with the decision of holding onto unforgiveness or choosing to forgive, and allow God to fill me with His peace and understanding.

I heard it said that unforgiveness is like a disease that suppresses the emotions we were created to express; it steals our joy and replaces it with resentment, our sadness with anger, and our peace with anxiety. And the sad truth is, we only hurt ourselves when we hold people ransom in our hearts for the things they did to us. Ephesians 4 tells us to, "Get rid of all bitterness, rage and anger, brawling and slander, along with every form of malice... forgive each other, just as in Christ God forgave you."

Now, I think we can all agree that forgiveness is hard, especially when you've been deeply wounded by someone or something. But I've learnt through my own life that forgiveness isn't a one time thing, it's a *daily* discipline that we need to put into practice. And as easy as it is to feel justified in your angry feelings towards those who hurt you, I was reminded on that evening around the table that revenge and justice isn't for us to decide; God has the final say in *all* things. Forgiving family members, exes, co-workers, neighbours or friends is not an easy thing to do by any stretch– it's often messy and confusing. But with the strength of Christ we can do it, while keeping our hearts set on the promise of freedom that Christ offers us through forgiveness. Forgiveness = freedom, and as tricky and complex as it may be, with the help of the Lord, will you choose forgiveness today?

TAKEAWAY

Examine your heart. Ask the Holy Spirit to bring to the surface those who need to be forgiven in your life. As hard as it may be, write down each name. Be honest with yourself because through this, you will begin to experience true freedom in Christ. If you're comfortable, bring your list to somebody you trust and have them walk alongside you in this. You don't need to do this alone– God cares enough about you and your heart to offer you this opportunity to choose forgiveness.

To The person
With Broken Dreams

I know you feel disheartened. The dream you once had just never came to pass. So, you've deemed it broken, lost and gone forever. Broken dreams result in a broken heart, and a broken heart creates a deep pain. It's a pain that you can feel in your chest, that brings you to your knees and keeps you in bed for days... sometimes weeks... sometimes even months.

Your pain, in the midst of brokenness, makes it feel like you've been forgotten, as though God doesn't care or perhaps He never has before. Oh, have I ever felt that pain before— it lived deep in me, consuming my thoughts, telling me I was a failure, that I wasn't good enough and that I'd never do the thing that passionately burned in my heart.

But friend, let me tell you that those are all lies. God does care, He always has and He always will— more so than you'll ever know on this side of heaven. You are not the author of your story, God is. Your broken dream is not the end of you and you have the chance to get back on your feet and dream like never before.

I know, I know, it's always easier to believe that the story God's writing for you is good when He says "yes" to your dreams. It's much harder to believe when He asks you to surrender them or decides not to fulfill them. Did it ever occur to you that maybe God was protecting you from something you didn't even know existed? Maybe He was refining your character in a way that could only be refined through the crushing and breaking of something you held onto so dearly?

Your dreams will be put back together in God's perfect timing according to His purpose and plan for your life, so place everything in His hands. Don't attempt to wrap your head around it all. Trust Him with all you've got, seek to move forward from your disappointment, and wait on God to give you hope for the future. Hope is at the core of your faith in Jesus; hope will heal your broken dreams.

Love,

Brooke
xo

"DO NOT LET YOUR HEARTS BE TROUBLED;
BELIEVE IN GOD, BELIEVE ALSO IN ME."
- JOHN 14:1 (NASB)

Comforter and Friend

"THE LORD IS CLOSE TO THE BROKENHEARTED AND
SAVES THOSE WHO ARE CRUSHED IN SPIRIT."

PSALM 34:18 (NIV)

It was the week before Christmas when one of my hometown best friends called to tell me that her Dad was in a terrible car accident and was hanging on for his life. The ache in her voice as she told me he was on life support, haunted me for months to follow. He passed away the next day. The feelings of pain and confusion that I felt that night were stronger than I'd ever experienced before; it was the kind of pain that made my chest physically hurt. But what I felt that night as I carried in my girlfriend's pain, was only a fraction of what I knew she was carrying.

We've all had our heart broken in some way– perhaps by disappointment, shame, rejection, or the death of somebody we loved a whole lot.

The shortest verse in the Bible is found in John 11 and it reads, "Jesus wept." This verse holds such power to me; it's a reminder that God doesn't leave our side when we are walking through the unimaginable, but rather, He is with us in our pain. As I listened to my friend cry countless tears over the phone that night, I was comforted in knowing that I wasn't the only one who cared about her heart. God cared about her broken heart and He was bearing all the emotions she was feeling, not only on that day but in the weeks, months and years to come. When we weep, He weeps with us. When we mourn, He mourns with us. 2 Corinthians 1:3 (TPT) says that God's character is compassionate: "He is the Father of compassion and the God of endless comfort. He always comes alongside us to comfort us in every suffering…"

The word "compassion" is the act or the capacity for sharing the painful feelings of another. Now, isn't that exactly who God is? I'm so thankful that God doesn't leave us to fend for ourselves but comes alongside us as our comforter and friend. Even when our hearts may be breaking into millions of pieces, there's comfort in knowing that God is near, bringing us the hope and healing that we need! The truth is, we may not always *feel* His presence during these difficult times, but thankfully our hope isn't found in our feelings but rather in *who* God is and the promises of His Word. The Bible tells us He is always with us, surrounding us with a tenderness that can only come from our Heavenly Father.

Whatever way your heart has been broken, know that God doesn't want you to stay broken and crushed in spirit. Instead, He longs to love you back to life and wholeness. In the same way that God was with my friend on the night her father passed away, He's with you right now in whatever it is that you're facing. I pray that you would invite Him into every area of your life that needs healing and hope, allowing His Spirit and Word to comfort you today. Whatever it is you're facing, know that God is close to you and loves you more than you could ever know.

TAKEAWAY

Take a moment to pause and consider how close God is to you. The Bible tells us that He's closer than the very breath we breathe. Delight in this truth and then ask the Lord to restore whatever relationship or dream has been broken, or whatever heartache from shame, rejection or disappointment you've experienced. Ask Him to take the pieces of your heart that have been shattered and put them back together in His name– into a new wholeness. God is nearer to you than the worry that rests on your heart and spirit; He is comforter and friend.

I will Praise you in The Dark

"YOU HAVE SURROUNDED ME ON EVERY SIDE,
BEHIND ME AND BEFORE ME, AND YOU HAVE PLACED
YOUR HAND GENTLY ON MY SHOULDER."

PSALM 139:5 (THE VOICE)

It had been a bad year to say the least. For 12 months, I was living in a really dark place and I didn't know if God was coming for me. Even though it felt counterintuitive, and was the opposite of what my heart and flesh wanted to do, I worshipped when it hurt and I praised through my pain. It ended up bringing me to a meeting place of just me and Jesus; a place I was in desperate need of. There were times when I wanted to give up, numb the pain, and erase the memories. But as I began to invite Jesus into the darkness, He met me exactly where I was and began to light up my heart with His unconditional love.

God's not afraid of the dark. Jesus suffered His darkest hour after dying the cruelest death, and having a stone rolled over His tomb. He endured this darkness so that when we feel abandoned and brokenhearted, we wouldn't have to fight on our own. The Bible tells us that God surrounds us on every side, and that even in our darkest times, we can experience comfort knowing that we are not alone.

Here's the cool thing about God: there's nowhere we can go that He isn't already. When our minds wander to those dark places and our souls feel like they're crushed at the bottom of the lowest valley, God's there, meeting us with His love and comforting embrace. Psalm 139:7-10 (The Voice) says, "Can I go anywhere apart from Your Spirit? Is there anywhere I can go to escape Your watchful presence? If I go up into heaven, You are there. If I make my bed in the realm of the dead, You are there. If I ride on the wings of morning, if I make my home in the most isolated part of the ocean, even then You will be there to guide me; Your right hand will embrace me, for You are always there." When we turn our hearts to God, we'll always have a father who loves us and cares for us in our time of need. No matter how dark our lives become or how alone we feel, *we will never be alone; for He is always there,* meeting us in our pain or isolation, and guiding us through every valley.

Worship is one of the ways we communicate with God (whether you sound like Celine Dion or a hungry cat); praising Jesus helps us to keep our eyes on Him, and off both ourselves and our circumstances. Will you invite Him into your darkest place today? Will you allow Him to meet you where you are in this season of life? I hope you continue to gain comfort in the truth that God never leaves your side and there's nowhere you can go apart from His Spirit. God's promises of strength for today and bright hope for tomorrow are neither empty nor subjective; they are for you, at all times. One night at my piano, near the end of that dark year, when I was met with the light of God's unconditional love, I wrote these words:

"I will praise You in the dark – I'll praise You when it's hard
I will sing through all the pain – there's victory in Your name
You God, You never let me go – You God, Your strength is all I need
to know."

May you praise Him when it's difficult, and when it feels counterintuitive, knowing that Jesus is near and is ready to meet with you wherever you are.

TAKEAWAY

Take a moment to sit and bring all that's on your heart before the Lord. Are you sad? Heavy hearted? Lonely? Having "dark" thoughts? God longs to meet you in an intimate place today. Who do you know God to be? Maybe you know Him as provider, your rest, the One who sees and knows you, healer, or friend. Sing the truth of *who* God is; let it echo over and over again as He meets you exactly where you are, lighting up your darkness with the light of His love and warm embrace.

I will praise you in the dark. I will praise you when it's hard. I will sing through all the pain. There's victory in your Name. You God you never let me go. You God, your strength is all I need to know.

ALL I NEED TO KNOW

[BROOKE NICHOLLS]

I Hear you, God

"WHOEVER HAS EARS, LET THEM HEAR."

MATTHEW 11:15 (NIV)

At the beginning of the summer, my friend called me to tell me that Bethel Music was having their big *Heaven Come* conference, and if I could get myself there, she could get us complimentary tickets. So my sweet husband who knows I *love* to worship, gathered all our points and flew me to Texas for a few days.

I went with great anticipation. It had been a while since I had been at a service as a patron vs a worship leader. This finally felt like a place to sit back, soak up the presence of God, and worship without having to think of much, or actually, anything at all.

Gathered worship is a guaranteed place of encounter with God— I always feel hopeful and expectant when I know I'll be gathering with the Church because if God's there (and He is), then I want a front row seat! As for Texas, I knew God was going to speak to me but I didn't realize He was going to say as much as He did. I chuckle, because, looking back, am I really that surprised? It's God! On night one God tenderly whispered to me, "You didn't need to get away in order to hear from Me." All I could think was, "Whoa, that's harsh." I tried defending and rationalizing this in my mind, explaining to God my schedule, pace of life, and everything I was leaving at home to come here. As if God wasn't already aware... Matthew 11:15 says, "Whoever has ears, let them hear." I really felt the Lord reminding me and convicting me of the truth that He will speak when I make Him a priority in my daily life. I don't need to go away to a secluded island, a retreat in the middle of nowhere— or in this case, to a Bethel Conference in Texas— in order to hear Him. He's given me ears to hear, I just needed to lean in. We *all* just need to lean in.

Yes, of course, silence and solitude are sacred and important for our spiritual growth, but it's not the only way to God's heart. As we get ready in the morning, as we eat our meals with our children screaming for more, as we interact with the people around us, and as we drive to and from work, God is *there* and He's wanting to pour into our hearts and ears. In our daily routines we just need to be actively listening, keeping our ear to His heart at all times.

God wants to speak to you today. He's not far from you and He's not silent. Don't wait until you're sitting under a palm tree, kid-free with your journal in hand, or when all of your work or extracurriculars are completed, because that time may never come. Lean in *now* and ask God *now* what He's trying to show you today. Make God a priority in your life as you remind yourself that you are not a slave to your schedule. Open your ears and let the sweet whispers of the Lord's love take you to new and higher places.

TAKEAWAY

Do you want to hear today? Do you want to feel God's presence knowing the new ways He wants you to see the world around you? Lean in and be active in your listening. Let's pray together.

LET'S PRAY

God, our gracious and heavenly Father, open our ears and hearts to receive Your truth in all its fullness today. I pray that our eyes would see the wonder of Your ways as we lean into who You are. God, speak to us in the busyness, speak to us in our sleep, and speak to us when we're least expecting it. In Jesus' name, amen.

Embracing The New

"FOR I AM ABOUT TO DO SOMETHING NEW.
SEE, I HAVE ALREADY BEGUN! DO YOU NOT SEE IT?
I WILL MAKE A PATHWAY THROUGH THE WILDERNESS.
I WILL CREATE RIVERS IN THE DRY WASTELAND."

ISAIAH 43:19 (ESV)

Fall is my favourite season. I love wearing jackets, sipping hot coffee, and smelling the leaves as they fall from the trees. This season comes with a bittersweet feeling though, because stepping into fall requires letting go of all the memories that summer held: the lake, the sun, and those warm nights spent watching the sunset over the city. I could hold onto those moments until the next summer rolls around, but by doing that I lose out on embracing the *new* season ahead of me.

Life can be viewed through this same lens: letting go of the old to free our hearts and embrace the *new* that God has next for us. Before we can move forward into a new thing, we usually have to let go of something that we've been holding onto. Embracing new seasons can be challenging because a *new* season doesn't always guarantee a *good* season.

I texted a friend who I hadn't chatted with in a while, asking her how she had been doing. She responded with, "It finally feels like spring has sprung in our home!" She went on to explain that she felt like she was coming from a long drawn out 'winter' in her family; she was joyfully and expectantly stepping into a new season God was bringing. She didn't like the 'winter' but knew God had been teaching her family many lessons through it and was gladly putting it behind her to accept the new that awaited them. Some seasons we walk into are positive and some negative, some wanted and some unwanted, some exciting and some terrifying; but as Christians, we have hope knowing that God goes before us in every single situation and season. Deuteronomy 31:8 (GNB) reads, "The Lord himself will lead you and be with you. He will not fail you or abandon you, so do not lose courage..." I don't know about you but I feel such peace in knowing that whatever I'm choosing to let go of, or whatever new thing I'm deciding to embrace, God promises to lead the way.

You're not alone in the familiar and you're definitely not alone in the unfamiliar. Isaiah 43 says, "I will make a pathway through the wilderness. I will create rivers in the dry wasteland." This is not only a reminder God declares, but a promise that He keeps. When we intentionally choose to believe God's promise of goodness in the new season, even if we didn't want a change of season, we can step into what's ahead with courage and an unsinkable faith. Whatever season you may currently be in, I pray that you would embrace it with a "God is in control" attitude.

TAKEAWAY

Consider all of the things in your sphere right now: your habits, your hopes and desires, your cares and concerns, your relationships, your fears, your circumstances, etc. If you're aware of the things you need to let go of, I encourage you to do exactly that. Hand them to God, giving Him full control. Ask the Holy Spirit if there's more you need to let go of in order to embrace the 'new' that God has for you.

In Him
I Can Do
All The
Things

"THE STRENGTH OF CHRIST'S EXPLOSIVE
POWER INFUSES ME TO CONQUER EVERY
DIFFICULTY."

PHILIPPIANS 4:13 (TPT)

The sun has barely risen– it feels like a dark winter day inside. Yet, the birds are beginning to wake up outside and I know I'll be kissed with the beauty of autumn in a couple short hours. Here I am, prepping for my day, my week and my month. My brain feels like it's spiralling out of control– so much in fact that I couldn't sleep last night. My to-do list is longer than I feel like I can manage, and I can't seem to find the hope of it shortening anytime soon. Three small words seem to be replaying over and over in my head… "all the things." I need to do all the things… Can you relate?

Let's be honest, we weren't created to do *all* the things. But don't worry, it doesn't end there because when God calls us into a season of "more than we're used to", He gives us the strength we need to get through it. And during this time, we need to be intentional about leaning into God's presence because this is when we are most susceptible to becoming worn out, burnt out, irritable, and the list goes on.

One of the first Bible verses my mom had me memorize as a little girl was, "I can do all things through Christ who strengthens me." (Philippians 4:13, NKJV) This verse made me feel so empowered as a kid, and I'm reminded that it rings just as true today as it did then. This verse partnered with wisdom is what we need to practice in the midst of a hectic schedule. Using wisdom is crucial when it comes to *"doing all the things…"* because like I said earlier, we simply aren't meant to do everything. So, what does that look like?

Sometimes we're required to give up certain things in our life in order to make room or manage a new pace (this is using wisdom). And sometimes, even after we make room we still feel overwhelmed, but there is a comfort in knowing that these seasons don't last forever. In Psalm 84:9 (TPT), the Bible says, "God, your wrap-around presence is our defense." So, whatever chaotic, frantic or overwhelming season you may be in right now, know that God is always with you, there to strengthen and protect you. You're not alone in this; lean into His wrap-around presence, knowing that He goes before you, behind you and surrounds you every moment of your day. I pray that you would know and feel where your strength comes from. Partnered with wisdom, through Him, you can do "*all the things.*"

TAKEAWAY

On the lines below, be honest with yourself and identify what season you're currently in. Is it busier than normal? Are you trying to meet deadlines that feel unmanageable? Are kids, work and your social life overwhelming you? Whatever it is, ask the Holy Spirit to show you how you can better 'settle into' this season. Are there things that you need to eliminate in order to keep peace in your spirit? Write down some things that you can do to help navigate during this time and ask the Lord for His wisdom and guidance as you do it. God is your biggest cheerleader and He's got you. You can do it.

_____

_____

_____

_____

Who God Says You Are

"BUT YOU ARE A CHOSEN PEOPLE, A ROYAL
PRIESTHOOD, A HOLY NATION, GOD'S SPECIAL
POSSESSION, THAT YOU MAY DECLARE THE PRAISES
OF HIM WHO CALLED YOU OUT OF DARKNESS INTO
HIS WONDERFUL LIGHT."

1 PETER 2:9 (NIV)

I've done a lot of things in my life that have tried to rear their ugly head in place of my name. Like: Brooke the wounded, Brooke the dummy, Brooke the insecure, Brooke the _____, fill in the blank. There are so many things in my life that I could allow myself to be identified by. But as a believer, I'm convicted by the truth that my identity is not in those things, but in Christ alone. Period. And because of that truth we all need to learn to see ourselves as Christ sees us, not the way the world or our inner critic says we should. I realize these types of statements are much easier said than done; but with the help of the Holy Spirit I *know* we can really begin to change how we view ourselves.

What names do you wear? Whatever they are, know that because of God's selfless act of love by sending His one and only Son to die for YOU, you are not defined by any those names. You're also not defined by the opinions of others, your circumstances, your successes or your failures. Instead, your identity is in Christ and who HE says you are. Your sin, your past, your mistakes, or bad decisions have all been nailed to the cross and God says that, *"you are cherished and precious in my eyes."* (Isa. 43:4 TPT)

I'm so thankful for a Father who doesn't keep track of our wrongs, rather day after day forgives us and reminds us who we are in Him. YOU are unfathomably loved by God in a way that is incomprehensible– I know you've heard this before, but stay here for a moment.

Stop.
Close your eyes.
Don't move past it.
Let your heart begin to tangibly feel His love.

Sit and allow this to sink in: God sent His child to die for *you*. He loves *you*. And the goodness of that truth doesn't stop there; God knew everything about you when He sent Jesus to die for you, and He chose you and continues to choose you every single day, regardless of how you view yourself.

Our identity is in who God says we are, but the question remains, "*who does God say we are?*" Well, the Bible tells us that in Christ we are:

Chosen, treasured, worth dying for, set free, set apart, and loved (plus a million more).

I pray that you would learn to see yourself as God sees you and trade in the names you once used to identify yourself for the truth of who God says you are. Let's shift our focus from how the world tries to define us and the lies it pushes us to believe about ourselves, and shift back onto this truth. Friend, you are *found* in Him and that can never be taken away from you.

TAKEAWAY

Read these verses from Scripture that truthfully describe who you are. Read them, rest in them, meditate on them, write and rewrite them down. Declare these truths over your life today as you begin to trade the names you've carried from your past for the truths of who God says you are!

You are…
- Treasured – Exodus 19:5
- Worth dying for – Romans 5:8
- Forgiven – Ephesians 1:7
- Set free – John 8:32
- Set apart – 1 Peter 2:9

- Made new – Colossians 3:10
- Seen – Jeremiah 12:3
- Known – 1 Corinthians 13:12
- Beloved – Jeremiah 31:3
- Chosen – 1 Thessalonians 1:4
- Called – Ephesians 4:1
- Made in His image – Genesis 1:27
- Healed – 1 Peter 2:24
- Reconciled – 2 Corinthians 5:18
- Made whole – Colossians 2:10
- A child of God – 1 John 3:1
- Adopted in God's family – Romans 8:15
- Not alone – Deuteronomy 31:8
- A masterpiece – Ephesians 2:10
- A Co-labourer – 1 Corinthians 3:9
- Delighted in – Zephaniah 3:17

I am chosen, not forsaken. I am who you say I am. You are for me, not against me. I am who you say I am.

WHO YOU SAY I AM
[HILLSONG WORSHIP]

Intimacy

"DRAW NEAR TO GOD, AND HE WILL DRAW NEAR
TO YOU."

JAMES 4:8 (ESV)

As the years come and go, I'm learning that setting resolutions doesn't need to be marked by a ball dropping at midnight and a new year; a fresh start can happen today. I don't know about you, but I've had, "go to the gym" as part of my daily goals religiously for probably the last 10 years. But let's face it, I've been like three times in the last 12 months (come on, I'm not the only one!). Thankfully, God is so graciously teaching me that the interior is much more important than the exterior. So I'll *gladly* trade in my daily goal of going to the gym with a daily goal to spend time with Jesus.

Have you noticed that choosing a "word" for your year has taken the place of resolutions? I went from making a list of 20 things that were, let's face it, never going to happen, to focusing on just one word or theme that would *actually* bring me closer to Jesus. Last year my girlfriend chose 'joy' which was the same year I chose 'pursue.' The coolest part about choosing a "word" for your year is that it doesn't stop after that year is done. Because when you intentionally choose to chase after let's say, *joy* for 12 months, that continues on in your days ahead becoming a part of who you are. So all of a sudden, it becomes less about *one* word and more about choosing *the way of Jesus*.

James 4:8 says, "Draw near to God, and He will draw near to you." What I've come to know through drawing close and spending time with God is that when we are *intimate* with Him, He'll take us to deeper places in His presence. After sitting with this verse the Lord kept speaking the word *intimacy* to me. At first, I was confused because I had been praying for wisdom and so I really thought God was going to give me that as my new "banner" so to speak. But as I began to draw near to Him in new and deeper ways, He revealed to me that when I stay in His presence

146

and grow in intimacy with Him, all of the things I pray for, including wisdom, will be found.

What are you asking God for? Are you needing peace in your life? Are you desiring wisdom? Or perhaps you are longing to hear from God more clearly. Spend your time focusing on becoming intimately closer with Jesus, then allow Him to fill you with the rest. I've learned over the years that the distance between Jesus and I is where the enemy can be found. The enemy will deceive us by telling us we're not ready, worthy, or equipped. But no, not today, Satan! We're closing those gaps and getting nearer to Jesus and the truth of who He is. God wants to take you to new heights today, tomorrow, and in the years to come. He wants to do incredible things in you and through you. He wants your heart and your whole life. So draw near to Him today; get cozy– because as you draw near to Him He will draw near to you.

TAKEAWAY

I encourage you to set a daily notification that reminds you to take some time getting intimate with the Lord. It can be 2 minutes, 5 minutes, 10 or however long you want! Set this notification to alert you at least once per day, maybe more! This can be hard with children and a chaotic schedule but trust me it will be worth it. Get up 10 minutes earlier if that's what it takes to quiet yourself in His presence. In this time with Jesus, ask Him if there's a "word" He wants you to lean into in this season. And remember, this isn't a race and it's not about the actual amount of time you commit to this, He just wants you! Keep this habit up and over time, be captivated by your closeness to the Father.

Jeremiah 29

"'WHEN SEVENTY YEARS ARE COMPLETED FOR BABYLON, I WILL COME TO YOU AND FULFILL MY GOOD PROMISE TO BRING YOU BACK TO THIS PLACE. FOR I KNOW THE PLANS I HAVE FOR YOU,' DECLARES THE LORD, 'PLANS TO PROSPER YOU AND NOT TO HARM YOU, PLANS TO GIVE YOU HOPE AND A FUTURE. THEN YOU WILL CALL ON ME AND COME AND PRAY TO ME, AND I WILL LISTEN TO YOU.'"

JEREMIAH 29:10–11 (NIV)

When I was in my early twenties I had a boyfriend who had "Jeremiah 29:11" tattooed in large cursive writing on his right forearm. This seems to be the Christian "go to" Bible verse when we need to be reminded that God has a plan for our lives. "'For I know the plans I have for you,' declares the Lord, 'plans to prosper you and not to harm you, plans to give you a hope and a future.'" What a beautiful scripture of hope and promise. However, we tend to miss the verse right before that reads, "You will be in Babylon for 70 years. But then I will come for you and do all the good things that I have promised, and I will bring you home again" (v. 10, NLT). Now, I wonder why he didn't have *THAT* Bible verse tattooed on his arm! (ha!) The reality for many of us is that we feel like we've been in Babylon for 70 years, and let's face it– nobody likes a Babylonian exile. It's filled with pressures, confusion and isolation which comes with many questions and doubts like, "why hasn't that thing come to fruition?" "Why am I still single?" "Why am I still in this place?" "How come I can't kick this feeling?"

So many whys, so little time.

Though our minds flicker and flutter around all these "whys," in the midst of our lowest valleys we need to cling to the hopeful Scriptures and promises of God's Word at all times. Your miracle may not come tomorrow, but believing God's promises above all else will provide you with the faith you require until that day. The truth is, we all have questions in our lives, and some of those answers won't be known this side of heaven. But as Christians we know *"that God causes everything to work together for the good of those who love God and are called according to his purpose for them." (Romans 8:28, NLT)* And because of this truth, we can go forth trusting His timing, His ways, and who He says He is.

149

Maybe you feel like you've been in Babylon for 70 years and you're losing hope. If that's you, I pray for increased faith to believe that God is with you in whatever you're facing. He is in control, He is sovereign, and He is preparing the way. He's in your marriage, He's in your trying, He's in your loss, and He is in your broken dreams. I pray that His faithful love would wash over you today, replacing discouragement with renewed hope. Your breakthrough is coming because you serve a promise-keeping God– one who promises to come for you, rescue you and bring you back home.

He is Elohim – The Strong Creator God
He is Adonai – Lord of All
He is El Roi – The God Who Sees Me
He is El Shaddai – Almighty God
He is Jehovah-Shalom – The God of Peace
He is Jehovah-Rapha – The God Who Heals

TAKEAWAY

Reflect on the pronouns of God shown above; which one speaks to you the most in the season of your life? Why?

_____

_____

_____

_____

_____

love lived out

"LET ALL THAT YOU DO BE DONE IN LOVE."

1 CORINTHIANS 16:14 (ESV)

On New Year's Day my Grandmother went home to be with Jesus. She was beautiful, and even at 96 years old wouldn't be seen taking a photo without her lipstick on (now I know where I get it from!). She lived a wonderful life and left her family with many stories that will be passed down from generation to generation. For the last nine years, I watched my Mom make multiple trips a day to the nursing home to make sure *her mom* was being fed, kept warm, and well cared for. She forfeited the comfort of her own life to make sure my Grandma, in her fragile state, was spending the rest of her days being unconditionally loved. The night she passed, my mom (at the age of 72) slept next to her on the ground so that she wouldn't die alone. This kind of selfless love has impacted me more than I can articulate because it wasn't motivated by her own needs, but instead, the need of another: my Grandma.

To love is to show deep affection for someone or something— an action that Jesus so perfectly embodied. The Bible is filled with stories of Jesus showing love at depths that are almost unfathomable. Whether it was healing those who were covered in diseases, feeding the 5,000 or extending compassion to the cultural outcasts— love was something that Jesus lived out daily.

1 Corinthians 16:14 says, "Let all that you do be done in love." Through the passing of my Grandma, this verse has come alive to me in a whole new light, because if I'm being honest, loving people has always come easy to me. It's just a part of my DNA I suppose, but I'm certain that if I stepped back and assessed the way I love others using *Jesus* as my example, I'd be pretty disappointed in myself. Love lays down its life for another, it sleeps on the cold ground to say its last goodbye and it pushes its own needs and wants aside to serve a greater purpose.

Today I pray that we wouldn't love simply out of convenience, but that in *all* things we would let love be our compass. 1 Corinthians is a great reminder to each of us that in everything, we are called to love without reason or boundaries allowing our head and heart to work together. May Jesus be our example of what it looks like to selflessly put our needs aside and boldly step out in love.

Praise God for tangibly demonstrating this kind of love to us through the life of Jesus. May God put us in more situations where we can step out and show this kind of wild love to the world around us.

TAKEAWAY

Using Jesus as your example, I challenge you to keep this idea of "living love out" on your radar this week. Watch to see what type of situations and spaces you may find yourself in and be aware of the way you are loving those around you. Are you motivated by your own needs or the needs of another? If there's an opportunity for you to go out of your way to show someone compassion (especially when there's nothing in it for you), I encourage you to let love be your compass and run toward it with all you've got!

The Things Above

"SET YOUR HEART ON THE THINGS ABOVE."

COLOSSIANS 3:2 (NIV)

Before I got married, I got dumped. Yup, that sweet bearded boy who's always beside me broke my heart into a million tiny pieces. But *wow,* what a blessing that was. Of course I didn't know it or feel it at the time because all I felt was an earth-shattering brokenness deep down in my heart *(because we all know every break up is this dramatic)*. But God always has a way of using our brokenness for His glory and our good, and that's *exactly* what He did. But before He began to put the pieces back together, I had a *very* big lesson that I needed to learn.

You see, I had my heart set on love and dreams, and while those things in themselves aren't bad, the way they consumed my every thought, was. The Bible tells us to set our hearts on heavenly things, and when we do that, things here on earth begin to align. So when my relationship ended (and my dreams died next to it) I turned to wanting quick fixes wherever I could find them. Basically, if anybody was having a party Monday through Sunday, I was there, and if it included avoiding my pain, even better. I filled my time with socializing, running from God and the truth of His word, and I spent way too much money on things I didn't need.

As embarrassing as this is to admit, I chased everything *but* Jesus, and in my pursuit, I learned that the things of this earth don't last; because they were never meant to. But when we turn our attention to Jesus and set our minds on the things above we become in tune with eternal reality, helping us understand what's *really* going on around us.

Philippians 4:8 was pivotal in helping shift my heart off the things of the world and onto the things above. It reads: "whatever is true, whatever is honourable, whatever is just, whatever is pure, whatever is lovely, whatever is commendable, if there is any excellence, if there is anything worthy of praise, think about these things." (ESV) Trusting and seeking God daily requires action on our part, because with all the worldly things that take up residency in our hearts and minds, we won't just naturally be drawn to always thinking "God thoughts." I pray that this verse encourages a shift in your life as you turn your attention to Jesus.

After a long drawn out season of learning to turn my eyes, heart and mind to Jesus, my life began to change. I began to see things through God's perspective and seek after what He desired for my life. Eventually my dreams began to take new shape and after much inner healing, that bearded cutie slid back into my DMs, and would later become my husband (bless up!). The hard truth is, sometimes God strips us of the things we love and that steal our attention in order to set our hearts back on Him.

TAKEAWAY

According to this verse in Philippians 4:8, do the "things" you give space to in your heart and your mind line up with the traits listed in the verse?

- True
- Honourable
- Just
- Pure
- Lovely
- Commendable

If not, ask God for help as you shift your focus from earthly to heavenly. Your focus is more than just a closet clean out; it's what allows you to recognize the love, nature, nearness, and work that God is doing all around you.

Turn your
eyes upon Jesus,
look full in His
wonderful face
and the things of earth
will grow strangely dim,
in the light of His
glory and
grace.

TURN YOUR EYES UPON JESUS

[HELEN LEMMEL]

to the person with Chronic pain

I can only write you this letter because of what the Lord has given me: eyes to see and, quite frankly, pain to feel. I understand the discomfort you feel as you lay your head down at night. The suffering you endure when you try to move your body, and the depletion of strength that comes from non-stop, all-day pain. You cope as the pain chips away at your joy, making you question everything you've ever known about who God is as healer, comforter, promise-keeper, and restorer.

Do you remember the story of Shadrach, Meshach, and Abednego found in Daniel 3? Basically, the Coles Notes of the story go like this: Three men refused to worship false gods because they knew that there was only one God worthy of worship. So, they got thrown into a fiery furnace– but before they got thrown in, they said to the King, "if we are thrown into the blazing furnace, the God we serve is able to deliver us from it… But *even if He does not,* we want you to know that we will not serve your gods or worship the image of gold you have set up."

Okaaaaaay, BUT EVEN *IF HE DOES NOT.* Talk about bold faith! There was zero doubt in their minds of who God was, and *even if* God didn't save them, they were still choosing to honour Him, serve

Him and trust that He is who He says He is. Do you see where I'm going with this? What if your healing never comes on this side of Heaven? Will you choose to put your trust in who God is? Will you choose to devote your days to Him? Will you believe that He's a miracle worker and healer?

I don't understand the degree of your personal suffering, but I trust in the One who meets you in the fire and walks through it with you. God is using your suffering for His glory, so keep seeking Him in your pain as He continues to reveal Himself to you in ways you could never imagine. And, though it's hard, keep leaning into His promise for renewed strength each new day. I haven't seen my healing yet and maybe you haven't either, but let's stand together in saying "YES" a thousand times to choosing to trust who God is in our lives.

"He will wipe away every tear from their eyes, and death shall be no more, neither shall there be mourning, nor crying, nor pain anymore, for the former things have passed away." (Rev. 21:4 ESV) Take hope today in knowing that one day you will receive your healing.

Love,

Brooke

xo

My Heart will Sing

"...SPEAKING TO YOURSELVES IN PSALMS AND HYMNS AND SPIRITUAL SONGS, SINGING AND MAKING MELODY IN YOUR HEART TO THE LORD."

EPHESIANS 5:19 (KJV)

With a coffee in hand and my laptop on my knees, I sat looking around the room. Where am I? What is this room? Oh, that's right… it's my new house. It still feels foreign, like I've been on a four-month vacation and will soon be returning to my micro-sized condo downtown.

It's been so busy the last little while that sitting down and breathing in my new digs hasn't been a reality for me, except for today. Right now in this very moment, I sit… ponder… take it all in. I hear God say "Go ahead…" but I don't know what that means. Go ahead and do what? "Sing the song in your heart," He says…

His whisper feels like a gift today– one I gladly receive. So here I am, asking myself, "what's the song my heart needs to sing right now?" Ephesians 5 reminds us about "…speaking to yourselves in psalms and hymns and spiritual songs, singing and making melody in your heart to the Lord." I've used this verse a time or two as a call to worship when leading a congregation, but today, it feels more like a personal invitation that is giving our hearts permission to sing over our season. And if you don't feel like singing today, that's okay too… pray it out instead!

So, what does your heart need to sing right now? What's going on in your life that you want to lift up? Perhaps you're struggling to know where to begin, don't stress… let me help:

Are you praying for rest? Matthew 11:28 (NIV) says, "**Come to me… I will give you rest.**" Pray it out.

Are you lacking joy in your life? Ephesians 5 (TPT) says, "**Be imitators of God… so your hearts will overflow with a joyful song to the Lord.**" Pray it out.

Are you looking for peace through your storm? Philippians 4:7 (NIV) says, "**And the peace of God, which transcends all understanding, will guard your hearts and your minds in Christ Jesus.**" Pray it out.

Are you needing hope through your trials? Romans 15:13 (TPT) says, "**Now may God, the inspiration and fountain of hope, fill you to overflowing with uncontainable joy and perfect peace as you trust in him. And may the power of the Holy Spirit continually surround your life with his super-abundance until you radiate with hope!**" Pray it out.

We all have a song in our heart; this song changes with the seasons and with the different circumstances that happen in our life. Sometimes our song feels non-existent, sometimes it feels buried in the chaos, and sometimes it's sitting at the surface ready to bubble over. When I first started leading worship, I would lead a song called "Forever Reign"; there's a lyric in the chorus that has always stuck with me that sings, "My heart will sing no other name Jesus, Jesus." The truth is, sometimes I have no idea what my heart wants to sing because there's just too much going on. Confusion, anxiety and fear have a way of blocking our words but nothing will come between our heart and the name of Jesus. So today, wherever you are, if your song is simply "Jesus, Jesus," let it be so, because His name is more than enough.

TAKEAWAY

Tell God how you're feeling today. Whether it be a song, a prayer, or a moment of journaling, let Him know the things on your heart. What do you need? What are you longing for? Is something weighing you down? Know that God meets you in your pain, holds you in your sorrow, and is the lifter of your head. He gives you the strength to walk through every moment of life, and He gives you the strength to sing the song in your heart today.

Carrying Out the Good News Of Jesus

"WE ARE THEREFORE CHRIST'S AMBASSADORS,
AS THOUGH GOD WERE MAKING HIS APPEAL
THROUGH US."

2 CORINTHIANS 5:20 (ESV)

I was driving to pick up a McDonalds breakfast one morning. Steve was still sleeping and I thought waking up to a greasy egg mcMuffin, and an even greasier hash brown would be the best start to his day (and I was right!). On the way there, I hate to admit this, but I accidentally cut off another car. As soon as I realized what I had done, I waved to indicate that I was sorry but I guess my wave wasn't good enough, because this car decided to swerve around me giving me all types of finger signals. In moments like these, it's easy to react (or in this case overreact), but how we respond really matters and says a lot about who we are, and who we represent.

I'm always challenged (in a good way) by this verse in 2 Corinthians 5 that tells us who we are as Christians. It says, "We are ambassadors of the Anointed One who carry the message of Christ to the world…" Now, the dictionary defines the word ambassador as, *"a person who acts as a representative or promoter of a specified activity."* What could be better than that?! An ambassador of Jesus Christ, responsible for showing His love and mercy to the world around us. I love that this is one of *many* truths that Scripture states about who we are.

As Christians, we carry the Spirit of God with us everywhere we go: to the grocery store, the office, into every gas station, and even when we're driving and somebody cuts us off. We represent Jesus, and being entrusted to be an ambassador of Him is a huge privilege and responsibility. I think if we kept this truth at the front of our hearts it would really challenge the way some of us interact with others. We carry out the good news of the gospel to the world, and as ambassadors how we live and respond to people matters. With this reminder that our responses matter, a change of heart, behaviour and actions should follow. In other words, how will you represent Christ when somebody cuts you off? Or better yet, when you're on the receiving end of all those finger signs?

Ephesians 5:1-2 (NASB) says to "be imitators of God, as beloved children. And walk in love, just as Christ loved you…" and in order to do this, we need to invite the Holy Spirit to come into our hearts and empower us to walk in this type of love only found in the Bible.

We live in a society that so desperately needs to be shown the love of God, not our quick and reactive responses. As you go out into the world today, I pray that God would deepen your understanding of what it means to be an ambassador, showing you all the ways you can practically live that out. Let us represent Him well, as He uses us here on earth!

TAKEAWAY

I invite you to ask God for the wisdom to know how to represent Him the best way possible to those around you. Pray that your words and actions would represent that of a loving, caring and generous Father. And by the empowering of the Holy Spirit, you would be able to tell a stranger how much God loves them, perhaps buy a coffee for somebody in line, or even ask your neighbour if there's anything they need prayer for. Never forget who you represent to the lost and hurting world around you today.

If The Stars were made to worship so will I

"THE HEAVENS DECLARE THE GLORY OF GOD; THE SKIES PROCLAIM THE WORK OF HIS HANDS. DAY AFTER DAY THEY POUR FORTH SPEECH; NIGHT AFTER NIGHT THEY DISPLAY KNOWLEDGE."

PSALM 19:1-2 (NIV)

"Look!" my husband yelled as he pointed to the sky. I stood wide-eyed. I couldn't believe it. We were both in total awe and wonder as green and purple filled the space above us. The colours danced across the night sky creating whimsical waves and swirls like I'd never seen or experienced before. Then, it hit me– I was having my first Northern Lights experience! In that moment– standing in the driveway in Saskatoon, Saskatchewan– I could feel the presence of God in the most beautiful, palpable way.

Have you ever felt close to God through an experience like this? I've heard people claim to feel His presence the *most* when they are out in His creation. Like me, maybe you've felt God while looking up to the mountains, walking through the woods, or breathing in the salty air blowing off the ocean.

God is omnipresent– wherever we are, God is there. Wherever we look, God's not only in it, but He's created it. California is one of my favourite places, and I always feel so alive the moment my plane hits the tarmac. I'm reminded of God's goodness when I feel the sun as it brings light and warmth into my life. The moon and the stars tell me of God's guiding hand as they light up the night, becoming these beautiful, burning heavenly lanterns. And the endless waves that wash up on the sand, day after day, remind me of God's constant love and mercy for me; a love that never runs dry.

I love the imagery and poetry found in Psalm 19:1-4 (TPT), "God's splendour is a tale that is told; His testament is written in the stars. Space itself speaks his story every day through the marvels of the heavens. His truth is on tour in the starry vault of the sky, showing his skill in creation's craftsmanship. Each day gushes out its message to the next, night with night whispering its knowledge to all. Without a sound, without a word, without a voice being heard, yet all the world can see its story."

This Psalm represents a moment where the author, David, stops in the middle of what he's doing because he finds himself completely in awe of God and all of his creation. I felt like David that night in Saskatoon. As I witnessed the colourful sky, I was reminded that God makes His goodness and power known through the wonders of His works. Never underestimate where you might meet Jesus– He's in everything and His presence will leave you in awe of Him.

TAKEAWAY

Now that we're all dreaming about Saskatoon Northern Lights and Californian mountains, take a look out your window and marvel at what surrounds you. He's in the blossoms as they bloom, the vibrant colours of the evergreens, and He longs to meet you as the sun sets in your very own backyard. I pray you would seek to know Him on a deeper level through His mighty works. Get outside! Go for a walk, a hike or even go stargazing! Let yourself get lost in awe and wonder at the beauty of God's creativity and the magnificence of His art. Then know that you too are one of His masterpieces.

If the stars
were made to worship
so will I. If the
mountains bow in
reverence so will
I. If the oceans
roar your greatness
so will I.

SO WILL I (100 BILLION X)

[HILLSONG UNITED]

Priority List

"COME WORSHIP THE LORD GOD WEARING THE
SPLENDOUR OF HOLINESS.
LET EVERYONE WAIT IN WONDER AS THEY
TREMBLE IN AWE BEFORE HIM."

PSALM 96:9 (TPT)

What is worship? Have you asked yourself this question before? As a worship leader, I've thought about this for years and have learned there are so many layers to answering a question like this. I really can't say I've landed on one specific answer. However, one answer in particular summarizes the priority we should give to worship as a spiritual discipline*:

> *"to worship is to honour with extravagant love and extreme submission."*

(*Note: Spiritual disciplines are practices found in Scripture that are designed to develop and strengthen spiritual growth.)

There are so many ways to express worship: giving, serving, singing and music, loving others and the list goes on and on and on. I read a book once called *"How to Worship a King"* (by Zach Neese) that really challenged me in my worship by saying, "True worship is a matter of the heart expressed through a lifestyle of holiness." Basically, our entire life is an act of worship. How we think, speak, work and live out our lives tells of where our heart falls into alignment with and submission to the Lord. And where we place God in our priorities is a real telltale sign of where our heart is, because *who* and *what* we prioritize is what we worship.

If you showed me your phone, I could show you what you worship. Your bank statements and a glimpse into your day, would show me the same. Now, I'm not trying to shame you, but rather open your eyes to the truth that we worship based on where we invest ourselves.

Don't you want your life to reflect the God you love and adore? Remember, like we just read, it's a matter of the heart– not just merely an act. Sure, you could go to church once a week and say that that counts– but hey, I get a bag of chips from the corner store at *least* once a week, but that doesn't mean I love and worship chips. See where I'm going with this? John 4:23-24 (TPT) is a good reminder of what having a true heart of worship should look like, "From here on, worshipping the Father will not be a matter of the right place but with the right heart. For God is a spirit and He longs to have sincere worshippers who worship and adore Him in the realm of the Spirit and in truth." "Spirit and truth" represent our priorities here, which could also look like this: *spirit and truth = who and what.* Spending time in the Word of God (truth) ignites our hearts to come alive which then causes us to come into alignment with His Spirit. God created us for the ultimate priority of worshipping Him– so making "spirit and truth" a part of our daily habits will transform our hearts, bringing us into closer relationship with Jesus. This worshipful lifestyle is what every single Christian should be chasing after.

Psalm 96:9 (TPT) reads, "Come worship the Lord God wearing the splendour of holiness." If your life does not display an extravagant love for God or the splendour of His holiness, then now is a great time to prioritize that. I encourage you today to make His name known by the way you live out your life so that He may be exalted in everything, honouring him with extravagant love and extreme submission.

TAKEAWAY

Grab a pen. On the lines on the next page, write down your top three priorities. It could look like:
laundry, kids, work.
OR: me, the house, friends.
OR: gym, healthy eating, husband.

As you go about your day, be aware of how and why you do the things you do. What's taking priority in your day? Is it God? Perhaps you need to shift some priorities around in your life.

I encourage you to make any necessary changes that may be standing in the way of making your life one that worships in spirit and in truth.

Position your heart, mind, and spirit in a way that allows all the things you do to become outward expressions of the truths you believe and of the One that you love. Build this mindset as each day passes and watch to see how worshipping in a way that's true turns out to be the root of everything you do.

_____

_____

_____

_____

Steady My Steps

"OH, THAT MY STEPS MIGHT BE STEADY, KEEPING TO THE COURSE YOU SET; THEN I'D NEVER HAVE ANY REGRETS IN COMPARING MY LIFE WITH YOUR COUNSEL."

PSALM 119:5-6 (MSG)

Over a decade ago, I was attempting to drive into downtown Toronto for the first time on my own. At that time, navigation systems were the newest, hottest item on everybody's Christmas lists– including mine. You know, the kind you lick and suction to your windshield? (Wow, that brings me back!) The problem was, I wasn't (and still am not) very good at using technology or following directions. I often think I can find shortcuts on my own and that my GPS will eventually catch up. I mean, naturally, I'm *way* smarter than the GPS. (And all the Enneagram Sevens out there said, "Amen!")

I was two hours deep into my drive when I realized I had been driving in circles around gravel country roads and could not for the life of me get back on track. Every shortcut I took brought me back to where I started. My gaslight was on, my bladder was full, and my phone barely had reception in no man's land. Finally, when I realized what was going on, I was frustrated, anxious, tired, and *very* over the drive... not to mention, I needed a gas station with a bathroom in a serious way.

John 16:33 (NIV) says, "In this world you will have trouble. But take heart! I have overcome the world." It's true, in life we will hit speed bumps, get in fender benders, and encounter some unexpected detours– those things are inevitable. But you see, God promises to give us His peace in those times, and reminds us that He is our "GPS". In other words, when we keep our eyes on Him, allowing Him to lead the way, He will lead us to a life of hope, fulfillment, and joy.

Sometimes we try to arrive at our desired destination by our own strength. You know, making decisions based on how fast we want to see things fall into place, being led by emotions or opportunity.

But God can't be outsmarted, and the shortcuts we try to take only hurt us and prolong where He is so graciously trying to lead us.

God is calling us to a life of righteousness and integrity; a life uncontaminated by the "things" or misperceived detours of this world. Psalm 119:5-6 reads, "Oh that my steps may be steady keeping to the course you set; then I'd never have any regrets in comparing my life with your counsel." When the world is telling you to go one way, and the Word of God tells you to go another, I pray that your steps would be steadily fixed on the course *He* has set out for you. And may you never look back with regret as you step into alignment with God's calling and word for your life.

God tells us that Jesus is our hope and that we are to trust His ways, even when we've gone off course, ignored the warning signs and lost our way. Take heart in knowing that God is the best GPS you'll ever need in life. Keep your heart set on His Word and your eyes fixed on Him as He leads you to new places today!

LET'S PRAY

Lord, we ask that You would lead us to a place of righteousness; a place where we are completely surrendered to Your will and plan for our lives. May we walk in agreement to all that You have set out for us, trusting in Your ways and leaning into Your word as our road map. You, Lord, are our strength and shield and we put all of our hope in who You are!
In Jesus' name we pray, Amen!

Anakainosis; the Renewing

"STOP IMITATING THE IDEALS AND OPINIONS OF THE CULTURE AROUND YOU, BUT BE INWARDLY TRANSFORMED BY THE HOLY SPIRIT THROUGH A TOTAL REFORMATION OF HOW YOU THINK. THIS WILL EMPOWER YOU TO DISCERN GOD'S WILL AS YOU LIVE A BEAUTIFUL LIFE, SATISFYING AND PERFECT IN HIS EYES."

ROMANS 12:2 (TPT)

In my early twenties, I was trying to find my way, like most twenty-somethings. I worked as a waitress, nannied, dreamt of starting my own traveling fashion truck, taught music lessons, and even started a wood crafting business. I searched high and low trying to figure out what God's will was for my life. I felt like I was wasting my days away and quite frankly, I was getting tired of it.

Have you ever wondered what God's will is for your life? In a world with so many choices, it can be easy to listen to the voices around us telling us who to be, and what to do with our lives. For me, I knew the truth of who God was but I wasn't necessarily living by it. I came to all my decisions from a mind conformed to what seemed acceptable to the world, rather than a mind transformed by the truth of the Word of God.

I love this word: *Anakainosis*. It's a Greek word that means "a change of heart and life; a renewal." But, how does one experience this type of transformation? Well, when we set our mind on God's Word, letting Scripture clothe our hearts, we allow the Holy Spirit to come and renew us from the inside out. Romans 12:2 (TPT) tells us to, "Stop imitating the ideals and opinions of the culture around you, but be inwardly transformed by the Holy Spirit through a total reformation of how you think. This will empower you to discern God's will as you live a beautiful life, satisfying and perfect in His eyes."

We tend to move toward what our mind and our hearts are fixed on. When our eyes are off Scripture, working in our own strength and understanding, we jump on whatever train is driving by (please don't make me rhyme off all my jobs from my twenties again). But, with our eyes fixed on God's truth, renewing us every single day, our wisdom kicks in and we're able to discern where God is actually wanting to lead us.

When we fix our attention on God, we are changed, period. Spending time in God's presence helps us to know His heart for us, and helps open our eyes to understand His way of thinking and will for our lives. Nothing will change us from the inside out like the Word of God will; this is where a *deep renewal* begins. *This is anakainosis*.

So, where is your focus today? What is your heart set on? Perhaps you need an *anakainosis*, a transformation of heart and life so that you can begin to know where God is leading you. My prayer for you today is that you would immerse yourself in God's truth with a mind and heart set on our Heavenly Father. May He direct your every step making clear His will for your life.

TAKEAWAY

Take some time to meditate on Romans 12:2 (TPT):
"Stop imitating the ideals and opinions of the culture around you, but be inwardly transformed by the Holy Spirit through a total reformation of how you think. This will empower you to discern God's will as you live a beautiful life, satisfying and perfect in His eyes."

- What does this verse mean to you?
- Are you living a life shaped by culture?
- Or are you living a life transformed by the Word of God?

Ask the Lord to help you discern what areas in your life need an anakainosis, and how you can move toward a reformation of how you think. The closer you become with God, the clearer you will begin to hear His leading. I pray that this anakainosis would bring you closer to God and further into His promises and purposes for your life.

My Help Comes From you

"OUR SOUL WAITS FOR THE LORD; HE IS OUR HELP
AND OUR SHIELD."

PSALM 33:20 (ESV)

I recently traveled across Canada to lead at a conference where I had the honour of meeting hundreds of lovely women. I heard story after story of "storms" rolling in, taking out entire families and turning lives upside down. Many women shared with tears in their eyes– some had hope, some weren't quite there yet, and some wondered if they'd ever be in the clear again. I flew home with these stories engraved upon my heart, encouraged with how God had shown up in these families lives and proved Himself over and over.

Through the stories that I heard, I was reminded of how common it is to lose energy, hope, and faith during the storms in our lives; feeling all alone wondering if we're the only one facing hardship. In moments like these it's so easy to grab at whatever we feel will keep us afloat and provide us with instant relief. Turning to our friends, the internet, substances, maybe our spouses... *and then* God. It is actually quite ironic because He's the only one on that list who can meet us in our hardships, and He never leaves us to pick up the broken pieces or fight on our own.

I think we've all been guilty of turning to things or people before turning to God in our time of need, and can agree that things would have turned out much differently had we just gone straight to the source of our help and healing. Psalm 33:20 tells us that, "...He is our help and shield." We have *direct* access to the One who offers us this help and protection, so we don't need to cling to anything other than Him. The Bible says that those who turn to God for help will have great confidence as they hold to the hope that lies before them– and God, being a strong and trustworthy anchor for their souls, will *lead them through the storm.* (Hebrews 6).

Just like in all of those stories, God wants to lead you through your storm today. Maybe you don't feel the hope that you need quite yet, and perhaps, you too, are wondering if you'll ever be in the clear again. But God is reaching out with both arms asking you to turn to Him with full confidence in knowing that He is your daily help and shield. Lift your eyes to Him, He wants to fill you with the peace and unspeakable joy to get you through whatever it is you're facing. Psalm 121:1-4 (NIV) says, "I lift up my eyes to the mountains– where does my help come from? My help comes from the Lord, the Maker of heaven and earth. He will not let your foot slip– he who watches over you will not slumber; indeed, he who watches over Israel will neither slumber nor sleep."

Take heart in knowing that God is your keeper and He will never forget or ignore you. Praying that you'd have renewed strength to lift your eyes to your maker today.

TAKEAWAY
Wherever it is that you listen to music, head there now and play the song "Cornerstone" by Hillsong Worship. Let the words of this song wash over your heart today as you declare that through the storm, He is Lord, Lord of all!

Christ alone, cornerstone.
weak made strong in
the Savior's love.
through the storm
He is Lord,
Lord of all.

CORNERSTONE
[HILLSONG WORSHIP]

Why Jesus?

"COME TO ME WITH YOUR EARS WIDE OPEN.
LISTEN, AND YOU WILL FIND LIFE.
I WILL MAKE AN EVERLASTING COVENANT WITH
YOU. I WILL GIVE YOU ALL THE UNFAILING
LOVE THAT I PROMISED."

ISAIAH 55:3 (NIV)

I was having coffee with an old friend who was sharing some difficult things happening in his life. In the thick of law school, he was feeling like the weight of his life was too overwhelming to carry on his own. Bobby knew I was a Christian, but never really asked too much about "church stuff" as he would call it. But at one point in our conversation, he turned and asked, "Why that Jesus guy?" to which I cheekily replied, "Why *not* that Jesus guy?"

What Bobby was explaining that afternoon was one of the *many* reasons *why* I chose Jesus. I grew up in a Christian home but I always felt like God was some*thing* I knew instead of some*one* I knew. I'd had encounters with Jesus before, but it wasn't until my late twenties when rough waters hit and I was left flailing my arms in need of some serious saving... and there was Jesus, comforting me, reminding me of my worth, and pouring His love upon me like a healing balm. I mean, He had been there all along, but this was the first time in my life where I met Jesus as more than a concept– I met my forever friend and Saviour.

Have you ever felt like the weight of everything happening in your life was simply too much to bear on your own? Almost like your human heart and frame just wasn't capable? Come on, let's read this invitation found in Isaiah 55 together:

"Is anyone thirsty? Come and drink– even if you have no money! Come, take your choice of wine or milk– it's all free! Why spend your money on food that does not give you strength? Why pay for food that does you no good? Listen to me, and you will eat what is good. You will enjoy the finest food. Come to me with your ears wide open. Listen, and you will find life. I will make an everlasting covenant with you. I will give you all the unfailing love that I promised."

What a beautiful invitation from Jesus to us. Offering spiritual water for the revitalizing of dry and dormant souls, spiritual milk for the nourishment and strengthening of weak lives, and spiritual wine for the delight and joy of sad and disheartened hearts. Friends, Jesus really is more than a concept– He's everything we need to face the waves. This here is the longer answer to Bobby's question that afternoon. *This is why I choose Jesus every day.* And I'll continue to do it a million times over because making it through this life on my own just isn't an option. We're not designed to rely on ourselves to get out of bed when depression and anxiety hits harder than imagined, or when guilt and shame tell us we have no place in this world, or when the weight of life falls on us all at once. We all have a ceiling we eventually hit, but the good news is that Jesus isn't limited by capacity. Will you accept His invitation today? Will you give Him your heart and life and allow Him to meet you exactly where you are, filling you with all the water, milk, and wine you could ever hope for?

TAKEAWAY
I want you to know that Jesus chose you when you were lost and insecure and He loved you when you couldn't love yourself. Today and everyday, I pray that you would choose Jesus exactly as you are, where you are, knowing He has already chosen you.

LET'S PRAY
Lord Jesus, we thank You for the gift of Your unfailing love and salvation. We pray that You would come and fill us with the

spiritual water, milk, and wine that we need. We invite You into our hearts and every area of our lives saying, "Have Your way in me Jesus!" Today we choose to do life with You as our forever friend and Saviour. In Jesus' name we pray, Amen!

God Says, "I am

"MY GRACE IS SUFFICIENT FOR YOU, FOR MY POWER IS MADE PERFECT IN WEAKNESS."

2 CORINTHIANS 12:9 (NIV)

I've been leading worship for many years now. I started when I was hardly a teenager, singing specials while the offering plate was being passed, and background vocals at youth group on Friday nights. Those were the glory days of using wedge monitors vs in-ear monitors and blowing out my vocal cords a minimum of once a week. Fast forward 20 years: leading worship all over Canada and into the US, opening for acts I used to dream of as a kid. Yet, somehow in the mix of it all I got caught up in the lie that I wasn't the right person for the job and began to feel so inadequate in what God was calling me to do.

Can you relate? Maybe it's in your job, your parenting, something in your personal life or relationships? How many times a week do you have thoughts like, "I'm not _____ enough?" (Fill in the blank).

I see people all over the place trying to find their self worth in others; looking for validation, strength, and confidence from one broken human to another. But that blank you just filled in cannot be found in other people, and the only 'person' we should be leaning on when it comes to our weaknesses is actually not a person at all, but rather God.

When you don't feel strong enough, God says, "I am."

When you don't feel secure enough, God says, "I am."

When you don't feel adequate enough, God says, "I am."

When you don't feel smart enough, God says, "I am."

God so graciously bridges the gaps in our lives and fills in the blanks with His "I AM." It's because of Christ in us that we are all these things– not because of anything we have or have not done. God fulfils everything we lack and everything that we need. 2 Corinthians 12 says, "My grace is sufficient for you, for my power is made perfect in weakness." What a great reminder that in our feelings of inadequacy and moments of weakness, the power and presence of God is made known in our lives. I pray you would trade in every lie that says you're not _____ enough, for the truth of who God says you are. Don't let the schemes of the enemy rob you of the joy that the Lord wants you to live in. Be free in knowing you are the right person for the job.

TAKEAWAY

Trading in the lies for God's truth sets us free. I pray that the lies that say you are not _____ enough will break apart from your heart and mind. On the lines below write down five truths of who God says you are and experience radical encouragement today as God says, "I AM."

1._____

2._____

3._____

4._____

5._____

a Well-Balanced life

"SEEK FIRST GOD'S KINGDOM AND WHAT GOD
WANTS. THEN ALL YOUR OTHER NEEDS WILL BE MET
AS WELL."

MATTHEW 6:33 (NCV)

The to-do lists seem overwhelming, don't they? Work, friends, church, our spouse, the kids, then the kids' activities, and somewhere, self care falls into the mix. Seriously, I could practically make this whole devotional a list of "to-dos." How on earth are we supposed to find sanity and a moment of serenity in the midst of such chaos? I guess a better question would be: How can we tap into living a well-balanced life that is honouring and pleasing to God?

I spend the majority of my time touring Canada leading worship for various churches, conferences and events; and when I'm not on the road, I'm at my home church. When people would ask me how things were going I used to say, "This is a busy season," but what I've come to realize is that *life* is a "busy season" and learning how to navigate it well has taken a lot of intentionality.

I was recently asked in an interview how I manage a well-balanced life. So, I want to share one thing that has been instrumental in helping me find that balance. But I also want to encourage you to find the thing that brings you balance and works for your own life. Something that brings you peace, fills you with joy, and feeds your soul. For me, it's community. Without the covering and grounding of our community, my husband and I wouldn't be able to sustain what we do on the road. Our community brings us a sense of rest. In fact, our community *is* our rest. Knowing that we have a handful of committed prayer warriors praying for us daily, holding us accountable and checking in on our marriage, keeps us on track and in tune with God's heart. In my personal experience as a Christian, this feels like an important marker for living a healthy, well-balanced life. Now, I'm not saying I do this perfectly– because I don't. But, I do seek out community with intentionality because it really matters to me. (I wish the gym felt as equally pressing, but hey... can't win 'em all!)

It can be hard to know how to get a handle on having a balance of work, play, rest and health. It becomes easy to worry about the days to come– even the days that have passed– but Matthew 6:33 tells us to, "Seek first God's kingdom and what God wants. Then all your other needs will be met as well." And isn't that so true? When we pursue God's heart, and make Him the centre of our lives, He gives us the wisdom to know exactly what we need in order to create balance and give us joy.

I want to encourage you to be intentional when it comes to living a well-balanced life because oftentimes, things don't just fall into place until we *intentionally* make Jesus the centre of things. Together, let's rest in the promise that when we seek the kingdom of God, He will guide us in truth, and the wisdom in knowing how to live a life of balance. Are you feeling like you could be doing this "balanced life" thing a little better? Well, hey– me too. I pray that God would reveal the things that are important to him, so that they would become important to you, and I pray that you would seek Jesus above all things; He will be your guide to living a healthy well-balanced life.

TAKEAWAY

What is something that brings you joy, fills you with peace and feeds your soul?

Write down a practical way that you could start living a more well-balanced life. Perhaps you need to add community to your list, better eating choices, or maybe quiet time with Jesus. Only you can answer this question.

On the contrary, maybe it's about elimination for you. Perhaps you need to eliminate something from your life that's interfering with you making choices to be intentional with your lifestyle. God cares about your well-being and wants you to seek out godly options to keep peace and joy a part of your daily state of being. Be honest with yourself as you take the first step to living a well-balanced life that's honouring and pleasing to God. You got this!

He's In the waiting

"REJOICE IN HOPE, BE PATIENT IN TRIBULATION,
BE CONSTANT IN PRAYER."

ROMANS 12:12 (ESV)

Recently, I went through a time in my life where I felt like something needed to break. I had been waiting nearly a year for God to show me what was next. I waited, I prayed, I cried, and I begged. But nothing. It took me months to understand that although my prayers weren't being answered the way I expected, they were still being heard. God was stretching me and refining me in ways I didn't know were possible; He was at work in *my* waiting.

Waiting goes against our natural human tendencies and culture really has a way of feeding into the whole "instant gratification" thing. In today's day and age, we don't have to wait for much and culture shouts back at us, "why should we?!" We have information, resources, and 'solutions' at our fingertips 24/7, including apps that allow us to have anything we want delivered to our door within hours. You want Thai for dinner? Coming right up! Groceries? Check your doorstep! Did you run out of toilet paper? No problem! Literally anything you could ever want, at your fingertips.

Being followers of Jesus doesn't necessarily work the same way. In fact, a lot of the things Jesus did seem backwards to the things culture thrives on. I'm reminded of the story in Exodus where Moses waited 40 years in the wilderness for God to come. 40 years! (And I thought I was doing good by keeping my cool in a 10-minute-long line up at Starbucks!). But surprise, surprise, God had a plan! He's not cruel, He didn't make Moses wait 40 years for the fun of it. He was making Moses wait because it was *in the waiting* that God was transforming Moses' character. Though Moses couldn't see it from God's perspective, God was doing the opposite of nothing. And what's even more encouraging? The same goes for us. God builds our strength and resilience in our waiting. If we fully trust Him in the process, our heads and hearts learn that He and He alone is all we need, and that He is actually preparing us for the coming fulfillment of His promise.

We all have dreams and desires that we want to see fulfilled. Maybe we have family members we've been praying for, or we wonder why healing hasn't come yet or question why we've been put in a certain situation. During seasons of waiting, we often feel discouraged because we don't know what to do with ourselves. It's so easy to feel helpless when we have no direction, but what I'm continually learning is that we need to be less reliant on our own doing and more reliant on what God is doing. Romans 12:12 (ESV) teaches us how to be active in the waiting season by telling us to, "rejoice in hope, be patient in tribulation, be constant in prayer."

My prayer for you is that you would rejoice with confident anticipation of all God has promised you. Believe that He's in your waiting; believe He's doing greater things than you could ever imagine. Although waiting can feel unnatural, I pray you would find comfort in knowing that God sees every one of His plans and promises to pass. Press into the presence of God in your waiting, trusting that even when you can't see it– He is at work in your life.

TAKEAWAY

It can be hard to wrap our heads around what we are or aren't supposed to do in waiting seasons. Being active in your waiting can look like: leaning into what God is doing by being open to the process, trusting Him, spending time with Him and returning to Him again and again. Although we may not understand what God is doing or what He has coming for us, it's important to trust His timing. Ask God to reveal to you **not only the outcome of these**

promises, but about your intimate thoughts and feelings during your waiting. Here are some questions you could ask Him in a season of waiting:

- What does patience look like in this season? How can I be patient?
- Is there something you're waiting for me to realize, to do, or to change?
- How do I discern a season of waiting from a season of what feels like distance? How can I recognize your nearness more in this season of waiting?

A Letter To The Person With a Broken Heart

The ache. The pain. The weight on your chest. The feeling of your heart being broken into a million pieces, as though it was ripped from inside of you and aggressively thrown to the ground.

It's hard to sleep at night when your mind can't stop thinking about that thing. You weep and wonder, and you ask God all the questions: Why me? Why us? Why this? Why now?

I was once told that a broken heart hurts more than the death of a loved one and although it's incomprehensible to think that anybody ever could understand your level of pain, I want you to know that God does. Psalm 147:3,5 (TPT) says, "He heals the wounds of every shattered heart... and he has infinite understanding of everything." Your broken heart isn't something you can heal yourself, nor are you left to. Wounds take time to heal and that healing can only come from God.

Friend, you are not alone. God sees your tears, He knows your pain and sits with you in it. He is close to you in your brokenness, pouring love and comfort into every corner of your heart. And in this very moment, He's holding every piece of it and He's holding the very thing that broke you.

I hope you find comfort today in knowing that God wastes nothing. I know that's a hard concept to grasp, especially right now because the pain feels too close and things are probably just too raw. I get it. But know that God wants to use your pain to help lead others into His presence. Your broken heart won't go to waste, and one day, your pain will be used to bring hope and healing to others who are experiencing the same ache in their hearts as you are.

So let your heart rest in the hands of God today as you take time to just 'be', and heal. Let your soul feel His presence as He surrounds you, loving you and caring for you in a way that nothing else could. God sees exactly what you're walking through and promises to be nearer than you could ever imagine— and by the power of Jesus, I'm praying for joy and peace to be restored in your broken heart today.

Love,

Brooke
xo

"THE LORD IS CLOSE TO THE BROKENHEARTED
AND SAVES THOSE WHO ARE CRUSHED IN
SPIRIT."
- PSALM 34:18 (NIV)

Your Love Never Abandons Me

"I HAVE LOVED YOU WITH AN EVERLASTING LOVE;
I HAVE DRAWN YOU WITH UNFAILING KINDNESS."

JEREMIAH 31:3 (NIV)

I sat across the table from my friend as he unpacked the last 10 years of his life. We ate some of Toronto's best carnitas and guac while he so graciously (and honestly) shared his story. Living a life so far from the Lord, caught up in addiction and chaos that had been marked by money, manipulation, and dishonesty... I couldn't believe the stories. As tears filled his eyes he explained his years running, hurting people and ultimately turning his back on who He knew God to be. Here's what got me though: his tears weren't because of the things he had done, but because of the way God had forgiven, redeemed and restored his messy life. He felt so undeserving of God's redemption but also so grateful for the grace and unconditional love he had been given.

I don't know about you, but to some degree, I can relate to his story. My friend's tears reminded me that despite our actions or the amount of years we've spent far from God, it's not in God's character to leave us or give up on us. He is kind and faithful when we are not, and His love is unconditional where ours isn't. He's the God of second, third and fourth chances and His love never abandons us; it's incomparable and eternal. The Bible tells us that He loves us with an endless love. You know, I'd like to think my husband will love me no matter what I do or say, but the truth is, he's human and he simply cannot love me in the same way God loves me.

There's nobody here on earth that will love us endlessly like God will.

I've been reminding my heart of this verse in Joshua 1:5 (AMP) where God says, "...I will not fail you or abandon you." Believe it or not, it never grows stale, because it's the truth. God doesn't leave us when we stray or make mistakes, and let's face it, if there's a time to let go of somebody, it's after they've strung you along and ignored you for years. But God doesn't see us in that light– He never sees us as too far gone. He's with us in our running, our straying and He so desperately wants to love us back into His arms.

It's easy to get wrapped up in our sin– in fact, that's exactly what the enemy wants. He wants us to feel too far gone, too unlovable, and too ashamed, reminding us of the things we've done and all that we are not. But our God who is love (1 John 1:4) calls us forgiven and chosen and follows us into the depths of our trenches, reaching into whatever place we're in, and loves us no matter what. And just like he met my friend with redemption and grace, He wants to do the same for you today. Rest in knowing that no matter the things you have done, the places you have gone, or the distance you have run, God's endless love will never run dry, fail you or abandon you.

TAKEAWAY

Think of all the places you've been or perhaps are in right now that feel 'too far' for God to extend His hand to you. Write these places down, and then, when you believe it in your heart of hearts, cross them out and write the truth over top that says: "But God won't leave me here." This process is not meant to be quick and easy, and the truth might be hard to believe. But the love of God isn't like any other love we encounter in this world, and through it all, He is with you and will not leave you.

CONNECT WITH BROOKE

brookenicholls.ca
Instagram: @brookenicholls
Facebook: facebook.com/brookenichollsmusic

Manufactured by Amazon.ca
Bolton, ON

15166988R00125